Reminiscences of an Archaeologist

Reminiscences of an Archaeologist

By
S.R. Rao

ARYAN BOOKS INTERNATIONAL
New Delhi

REMINISCENCES OF AN ARCHAEOLOGIST

ISBN-10: 81-7305-351-0
ISBN-13: 978-81-7305-351-1

First Published in **2008** by:
ARYAN BOOKS INTERNATIONAL
Pooja Apartments, 4B, Ansari Road, New Delhi-110 002 (India)
Tel.: 23287589, 23255799; Fax: 91-11-23270385
E-mail: aryanbooks@vsnl.com

Computer Typeset and Printed in India at
ABI Prints & Publishing Co., New Delhi

Preface

India has as many as 5,000 monuments of national importance and 50,000 of regional importance, the custodian of which is the Department of Archaeology at the centre and in states. Besides the conservation and presentation of this great cultural heritage in a meaningful way to the common man, the archaeologist has undertaken research by way of excavation of sites on land and in the sea in order to fill the gaps in Indian History. Unfortunately, the western scholars have dubbed these gaps as the dark age of Indian History mainly because they think that tradition may not be an important source of history.

True, a researcher in history and archaeology cannot simply accept tradition as history, nor ignore it totally. I give an example of my own experience

During my excavation of the important site of Lothal, an Indus Civilization site, in 1955-1962, I ignored the tradition that the warehouse mound was considered as the seat of the Sea Goddess (Vanuvati Mata) and started excavating it. After an accident, the labourers refused to work as they thought the ancient Goddess was disturbed. Actually on further excavation, we found the famous dockyard, the largest structure of its kind.

This does not imply that the archaeologist has to accept in toto the tradition. He has to separate the grain from the chaff, as I had to do in the case of Dwarka about which there are hyperbolic references in literature. But the location of Kusasthali, Dwarka and Gomati Dwarka mentioned in literature are correct. The town plan found in excavation agrees with literature.

There is also a difference in the dates assigned to Dwarka (3102 BC) according to tradition and 1800 BC according to T.L. dating and C14 dating methods. There are other supporting evidences for scientific dating namely two inscription in evolved Indus script and Sanskrit language, a unique seal for identification of the citizens of Dwarka mentioned in Mahabharatha. The above instances suggest that a researcher should be cautious in dating.

Of late, the archaeologist is reluctant to take decisions needed for the preservation of Indian's cultural heritage primarily because the department is headed by a non-specialist. It is high time that the recommendations of the expert committee appointed a few years ago are implemented immediately. There is no dearth of funds nor talent and it is an action that is needed.

I have keenly felt the need for obtaining the cooperation of the public in solving certain problems which the archaeologist has to face. In fact, if he is sympathetic to their requirements and if explained in a concerning way, I feel the people are not only cooperative but also enthusiastic to help the archaeologist as in the case of the land needed for Lothal Museum.

As many colleagues of mine and the public wanted that I should reduce to writing my experiences in on-land

and under-sea excavations as well as conservation of various types of monuments such as the Taj Mahal, Ajanta Caves, Chalukyan Temples, etc., I have made particular mention of their problems of conservation.

I am grateful to Shri Vikas Arya of M/s Aryan Books International, Delhi, for having come forward to publish this "Reminiscence of an Archaeologist" and done a very good job of it.

My thanks are due to all my colleagues in the Archaeological Survey as well as State Archaeological Departments and to all the scientists in NIO, Goa, for extending cooperation to me to make my work easy.

I am also obliged to my family members mainly Kamala (wife), Gopal (son), Meena (daughter-in-law) and daughters Nalini and Shakuntala for their continued help in my work.

Bangalore **Shikaripura Ranganatha Rao**
24-4-2008

Contents

List of Illustrations

1

Childhood and School Days

With an eight-day-old baby in her lap, the frightened mother Kamala Bai seated in her bed on a wooden cot in the mud-walled house of the village, Anandapuram in Sagar Taluk of Shimoga district in Karnataka is dumbfounded. She is silently watching three masked robbers carrying away two wooden boxes and a steel trunk at midnight from the adjoining room. Five other children of hers, Narayana, Ramachandra (Moti), Srinivasa (Seena) – all boys, Sita and Tunga (girls) were fast asleep on the beds spread out on the floor. Kamala Bai's aunt Radha, pregnant and half-asleep, would not dare move. After 30 minutes, both shouted for help and their Muslim servant, Sabu, sleeping in the verandah, reluctantly got up and asked Kamala Bai what the matter was. On being told that thieves had entered the house and had taken away the boxes, Sabu lit up a lantern and started looking for the thieves in the dark. The village police outpost being a few furlongs away, it took some time for a police constable to reach their house. He and Sabu went into the thick forest behind the house and could find only three empty boxes broken open by the thieves. Early morning at 6 a.m. a messenger went to Jog Falls, one of the highest waterfalls in the world, where the River Sharavati takes a 900 ft leap from the precipice of the Western Ghats, part of the Sahyadri range of hills. Here Kamala Bai's husband Hucha Rao, a revenue inspector, was camping for making arrangements for the visit of a high dignitary in the Viceroy's Secretariat of Delhi. That was the time when the British were at the height of their power in India. The previous night, Hucha Rao had a dream in which the god, Ranganatha, a Vaishnava deity of the temple at Anandapuram, had appeared almost naked except for a *langoti* (loincloth) and beckoned him with a sarcastic smile. When Hucha Rao heard the news of the theft in his house which had made him a pauper, he thought that the dream which he interpreted as reducing him to chill penury, had come true. He rushed to Anandapuram on his horseback. While ascertaining details of the loss, he came to know that the thieves, who were hiding behind the wall the previous night had overheard the conversation between Kamala Bai and Radha giving details of the jewels kept in three boxes. That was a sufficient inducement to the thieves to enter and take away the boxes especially when the revenue inspector was on tour.

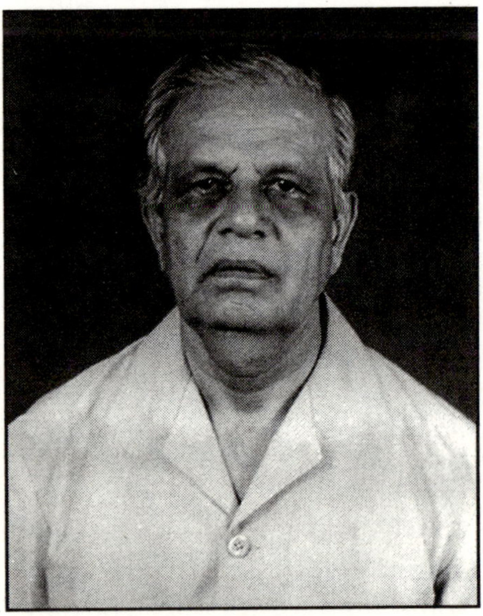

Fig. 1. Author.

Fig. 2. Parents of Author, Kamala (left) and Hucha Rao (right).

On the tenth day of the birth of their newborn child, it was named Ranganatha (Fig. 1) after the tutelary deity of the village, a tradition which (Fig. 1) the parents (Fig. 2) did not want to ignore. That is how the sixth child (fourth boy) came to be later known as Shikaripur Ranganatha Rao (abbreviated S.R. Rao, the author of the autobiography). Shikaripur was the name of the place to which Hucha Rao belonged. One may wonder why the boy's father was called 'Hucha' which literally means 'mad or indigent' in Kannada language. The reason is not far to seek. Just as Ranganatha was the name given to the newborn boy after the tutelary deity, his father had been named 'Hucha' (*bhrānteśa*), which is the nickname of the tutelary deity of Shikaripur, namely, Anjaneya (Hanuman), the greatest devotee of the epic god, Rama.

Coming back to the theft, it appears that after much effort the police were able to catch the thieves who had come from Bellary district, one of the richest districts of the Vijayanagar empire in the 14th-16th century but was reduced to a desolate town of poverty and misery after the sack of Vijayanagar city by the invading Muslim armies of Bijapur soon after the battle of Talikota in AD 1565. Besides looting the temples and residences of their riches, wholesale massacre of the population and burning of the temples had taken place. Struck by fear and having lost all means of living, the few suriving residents left the city.

I grew up under the care of my parents and was always eager to listen to stories narrated by my father. Two stories are still fresh on my mind – one of the court jester, Tenali Ramakrishna and the other about the rise and fall of Vijayanagar. It may not be out of place to mention here what the foreign historians of Vijayanagar had to say in the matter of destruction of the capital (*The Fall of Hampi*, January 1565),

> Never perhaps in the history of the world has such havoc been wrought and wrought suddenly on so splendid a city, teeming with a wealthy and industrious population in the full plenitude of prosperity one day, and on the next seized, pillaged and reduced to ruins, amidst scenes of savage massacre and horrors beggaring description (R. Sewell, quoting a 16th century traveller in *A Forgotten Empire (1900)*. Earlier a Portuguese traveller to Vijayanagar (1520-22) wrote "what I saw seemed ... as large as Rome and very beautiful to the site ... the best provided city in the world."

Subsequent to the fall of Vijayanagar, Bellary district witnessed famines periodically, which in turn forced the unemployed landless labour population to take to dacoity. It is only during the last three or four decades, irrigation of land fed by the Tungabhadra channels has helped the development of agriculture.

The family background of my father, Hucha Rao throws some light on the social and economic condition of some remote villages. Hucha Rao lost his father Raja Rao when he was fifteen. His mother and elder brother lived in Danavasa near Narasimharajapuram in Chikmagalur district. He was a coffee planter with a small estate and fifty heads of cattle. Coffee seeds being very cheap in those days, there was no substantial income for the family. For a Brahmin, education being the mainstay, Hucha Rao not only had his general education up to first year in arts with English and Mathematics as main subjects, but also studied law hoping to fulfil his ambition of becoming a lawyer. Unfortunately, by the time he completed the course, rules were changed. A degree was essential to practice law. As he was married, he had to seek a job to sustain the family in Shikaripur and got the post of revenue inspector on a salary of Rs. 15 per month. My father had to look after four uncles of mine also for sometime. Even when he was posted to various places, where there were no good schools, he took great pains to educate his sons. My eldest brother, Narayana Rao obtained his B.A. degree with English, Sanskrit, History, Economics, and Logic as main subjects during a 4-year course (2 years in intermediate college and 2 years in a degree college) from the University of Mysore. This was considered a crowning achievement for the family. Unfortunately, government jobs were few. However, after one or two years of waiting he got a temporary post of a clerk in the district office at Shimoga. After it was abolished, he took to teaching and became a teacher in Sanskrit in the Middle School at Shimoga in the year 1931. My other two brothers did not fare well in studies; Ramachandra passed high school examination and later entered the Mysore Iron and Steel Works at Bhadravati as a daring mill-hand. In fact, I was astonished to see how he could push the red hot steel billets in the steel mill. Although Brahmin boys are too soft and reluctant to take up such arduous jobs involving manual labour, Ramachandra (nicknamed Moti) took it as a challenge and succeeded in pleasing his German bosses, Henz and Babart. After the Second World War broke out in 1939, both the Germans were in detention and my brother forsook his job and took to ministerial work in the Indian

Coffee Board at Bangalore. My next elder brother, Srinivas who was reluctant to study English, preferred training in carpentry in the Government Industrial School and later proved himself an excellent supervisor in the pattern shop of Mysore Iron and Steel Works and Hindustan Aircraft, Bangalore. The above brief account of the education and professional careers of Brahmin boys of the early thirties and forties of the last century disproves that certain castes were forbidden from following a trade other than the one prescribed by custom. About my own education, I have many things to say.

As was the custom, my father taught me orally the names of the *tithis* (days in a fortnight), months and years according to the Hindu calendar and also the multiplication tables. I could recite Sanskrit *slokas* (verses). My father had learnt Sanskrit and Marathi in order to learn Astrology. I studied Kannada for four years in the primary school at the village known as Jade where my father was posted. During the holidays, I used to go with him to various villages in a bullock cart. He had to maintain a horse also, which he did and was a good rider too.

My mother who had a sonorous voice and was a very good singer had taught me a song in praise of Krishna. I enjoyed listening to devotional songs in Kannada sung by my mother. She could also recite almost the entire ten *adhyayas* (cantos) of Sri Venkatesa Parijata, the story of the marriage of God Venkatesa with Padmavati in verse sung especially during the Dussehra festival. My sisters and I learnt the *raga* and *tala* of the songs.

During one of his itineraries, my father took me to a place called Banavasi (Vanavasi), the ancient capital of the Kadambas who ruled the coastal region about 2000 years ago. There is a beautiful temple of Madhukesvara here. At the car festival of the god every year, a chariot is decorated with buntings to take the images in procession. My father told me that originally the canopy of the chariot was more than 50 ft high but it was reduced at the behest of the Englishman, perhaps the collector (deputy commissioner) or some other official, whose hat fell down when he looked up at the chariot. This may or may not have been true, but the story made a great impression on my young mind. I used to remember Banavasi temple not for the chariot but for its beautiful sculptures.

After completing my studies in the primary school at Jade, I had to go to a town where there was a middle school. Before doing so, my father taught me the *mantras* of daily prayer (*sandhya vandana*) and worship of God (*Deva puja*) and got me initiated as a Brahmin by performing my *upanayana*. My father was a great disciplinarian and a true educationist. But for his insistence on learning Sanskrit in which he was an expert, I wonder whether I would have done well in discharging my duties as an archaeologist in later life. He made his sons learn by heart important *slokas* from Kalidasa's works *Sakuntalam, Meghaduta* and *Kumara-Sambhava*. He used to say one should aim high to achieve great objectives in life. *"Nocchārtho viphatlāstu dūshaṇapadam dūshyāstu kāmolaghuh."* One is not to be blamed if one aims high but fails despite efforts to achieve it, but one is to be blamed if the aim is low. He was a nationalist and could meet any challenge. Although he was in the service of the government of Mysore, which was pro-British, he subscribed to the nationalist *Daily Kesari* edited by Bal Gangadhar Tilak. He used to explain to the family members and the villagers the details of the rise of the national movement and Gandhiji's *Satyagraha* in Africa. It is this kind of early education at home which went a long way in moulding my life.

As there was no middle school at Jade, I had to leave my parents at the age of 8 to go to Shimoga town for pursuing my studies further. I lived for one year with my maternal uncle Satvik Krishna Rao who was very affectionate. His wife, Radha Bai was like a mother to me. I must also mention here how deeply I was attached to my friend and classmate, Babu as he was affectionately called. One day his grandmother objected to my going to his house to play with him. I was upset, did not talk to anyone and wept all night. I came to know that Babu also did the same. The next morning, his father brought Babu to my house. Immediately, we embraced and wiped the tears of each other. After a few months, his father, a chief officer of the town, was transferred from Shimoga. My uncle lived in a part of a large European bungalow on the bank of a large irrigation tank known as 'Angleyaṇa Kere' (meaning in Kannada Englishman's tank, perhaps because he got it repaired). When my father and mother came to Shimoga we settled down in another part of the same bungalow, which had a very large mango grove in front and a small pond in it. My most favourite fruit is mango, rightly called the 'king of fruits.' My favourite sport was swimming in the sacred River Tunga which cascades through boulders near Shimoga, and slowing down five miles downstream at the village of Pillangeri, finally joins the River Bhadra at Kudali. Thereafter, the river is named Tungabhadra on the banks of which the capital of the Vijayanagar empire was built. From the very beginning of my middle school days in 1929 until I left for my college studies in Mysore in 1936, I enjoyed swimming in the crystal clear waters of the Tunga in winter and summer; but I dared not swim in floods. This was the privilege of my daring brother, Seena. He would jump from the 10-ft high stone pavilion into the swirling waters of the flooded Tunga and dive and disappear for a minute or two causing great anxiety for me whether he would come up alive or not. Swept by the flood current he would surface one furlong downstream and then walk back shivering in cold to tell me how he extricated himself from the whirlpool. Though he had strictly warned me not to tell my father about his adventure, I could not suppress my feelings of disaster overtaking my brother in his wreckless adventures. He got a good beating from my father, but this never prevented us from swimming in safer waters under the railway bridge. I too was given a mild thrashing by my eldest brother, Narayana for swimming for too long, even forsaking my lunch. I realised later how dangerous it was to swim during floods, when Narayana's son Badari was drowned in the River Tungabhadra at Kudali. Kudali was one of our favourite holiday resorts in summer, especially in the month of *caitra* (April) when the car festival (*rathotsava*) of Lord Venkatesa is celebrated with great pomp. Thousands of pilgrims flock to this place. Some walk long distances and others come in bullock carts and horse-drawn carriages from Shimoga. On that occasion, one of the disciples of the pontiff of the *matha* undertakes free feeding of the poor.

My father thought that one day Hindi may become a national language, so he asked me to take it as an optional (third language) subject in High School for the SSLC (Secondary School Leaving Certificate) examination. There were about 20 boys in the Hindi class and we had the unique distinction of having Sri Markandeya Rao, a tall, fair gentleman as our Hindi teacher. He had passed the highest Hindi examination from Banaras Hindu University and loved to teach Hindi to us. It should be said to the credit of the Department of Public Instruction in Mysore that in the early thirties teaching Hindi as an optional subject was part the curriculum. Markandeya Rao used to make us tell stories from the book *Majedar Kahaniya*. Another text was the drama *Durgadas* – the thrilling story of a brave Rajput prince who fought for the freedom of his kingdom Mewar in Rajasthan. This was at a time when Rana Pratap and other Rajput kings were fighting against the Mughal Emperors

Akbar and Aurangzeb. At the school day function, I took part in the drama *Durgadas*.

Strict discipline was maintained in the classes and school premises. When Dr. T.N. Jacob was the headmaster his son did not return on schedule from Mysore immediately after participating in the state Dasara cricket matches. He came next day, but Jacob did not allow him to attend the classes, made him stand in the sun for an hour and chided him for absence without permission.

As a freeship holder in the first two years of my high School days I used to score high marks. At the end of the second year (V Form), I was confident of scoring high marks in the annual examination to earn a freeship next year but an incident unnerved me. The school's close proximity to my house made it possible for me to hear the morning prayer. On the day the mathematics paper was to be answered, I thought the examination would start as usual at 10:30 a.m.; I was still reading in the upper storey of our house. When my mother, who heard the ringing of the school bell and the prayer, told me that the examination may begin at 8 a.m., a warning which I ignored. When I went to the school at 10 a.m. with great enthusiasm to take Mathematics paper, I was shocked to find my classmates returning home after answering the paper. Nothing worse could have happened to me because it is in Mathematics that I used to score highest marks (almost 95 to 96 per cent) to make good the loss of a few marks in other subjects. I ran back home and started weeping. My father scolded me and at the same time encouraged me to meet the Headmaster Mr. Sangameswaran and tell him how I missed the examination and that it may result in the loss of my freeship. The headmaster, who is usually angry with students who advance excuses for failure, was kind enough to tell me that the committee will take into account my performance in other subjects and also in the previous examination. I thanked him but still unsure of getting the freeship went home. Later I was listed among merit students and awarded freeship which meant exemption from paying a fee of Rs. 3 per month.

My father was carefully monitoring my performance in the monthly tests and mid-term examination in VI Form (final year of high school). He made sure that I score high marks in English, Sanskrit, Mathematics, Science, Hindi, and Geography. I used to go in the evening for study in the cool breeze of the River Tunga carrying with me some raw mangoes, salt, jaggery and chilli powder to make an instant pickle and eat it now and then. At sunset, I used to offer prayers to Sun God Suryanarayana and Goddess Sarasvati and also perform my evening *sandhya vandana* in the river. Back home, after a light meal, I used to study in the dim light of an oil lamp; Shimoga town did not have the 'luxury' (later a necessity) of electricity in those days.

I did play games in my high school days, but having hurt the ringfinger of my right hand on the very first day of playing cricket, I swore not to play cricket anymore. I took to football for a couple of years in the school. I liked scouting and joined the mini scout brigade, which brings to my mind the camp fires organised in Shimoga and nearby villages. We, young boy scouts, were asked to enact *Mouglis Hunting* of Rudyard Kipling which included a scene of hunting and skinning the tiger, the cattle-eater. Later, I read Kipling's works. He wrote, "East is East, West is West, never the twain shall meet." The reaction of Indians to this poem is too well known to be repeated here.

I did well in final SSLC examination and spent summer holidays in visiting some nearby places of pilgrimage such as Pillingeri, Kudali and Eḷuśiḷu (where Tunga River is split into seven streams *(śīḷu)*. One day at 10 a.m. in April 1936, I was told that SSLC examination results were announced.

I rushed to the school and eagerly looked up the notice board. The teacher told me that I had passed. I spent an hour or so brooding over my result in II class and then came home to tell my father the rather unsatisfactory results. He laughed and told me that there are only two first classes for the entire Shimoga district and mine was one. The other student who got a first class was my friend Gurumurthy. I jumped in joy. Everyone in the house was happy. The news spread like wildfire among friends and relatives. Sweets were distributed, after offering prayers in the Anjaneya (Hanuman) temple in the fort.

Although my teachers and parents were anxious that I should continue my studies, there was no hope of going to a college in Mysore. The greatest worry of my father was to find money for books and my boarding and lodging charges in a college hostel at Mysore. He could not afford it. Day in and day out he started consulting his lawyer friends, but there was no monetary help from anyone. It is at such an hour of great need, God does help those who deserve it. A weaving master who used to come to our house and understood my father's worries suggested to him that he should try to admit me in the *Anathalaya* (orphanage), a free boarding home for poor Brahmin boys in Mysore. My father could not think of an orphanage for his son, but he overcame that feeling of helplessness and made serious efforts to take me to Mysore and try for admission in the *Anathalaya*. He collected a hundred rupees for initial expenses including tuition fee, books, etc. My maternal uncle Seshagiri Rao, a railway guard, got me a free passage to Mysore. Another uncle Nagaraja Rao, who was undergoing training in undergraduate teachers training course in Mysore, accommodated us in the hostel. There were about three others from villages who had passed SSLC in 1st class from high schools in Hassan, Mandya and Tumkur districts. I was the only one from Shimoga and that too a 1st class student which went in my favour. This was the turning point in my career and my father was excited about it. He blessed me, gave a small amount for fees and books and reluctantly went back to Shimoga. My mother, though sorry to find her son staying in an orphanage, was pleased to learn that I could continue my studies.

Before I narrate the events relating to my studies in the college and about *Anathalaya,* I must mention the name of a great poet who influenced me when I was a student in the high school. He is Dattatreya Ramachandra Bendre, a renowned poet of Karnataka who had the pen-name Ambikatanaya (son of goddess Ambika). He was known for composing poems extolling the freedom movement in India and exhorting the youth to fight peacefully for procuring India's freedom. He visited Shimoga high school in 1935 and sang in his sonorous voice the famous song *Makkalivarenamma muvattumurukoti.* Are these 33 crore people the children of *Bharata mata* who is groaning under the shackles of foreign rule? Let them rise to free Mother India from bondage.) Inspired by him, I joined the morning demonstrations *(prabhat pheri)* of the freedom movement led by another student Ananda, son of a lawyer, K. Srinivasa Rao. In the evening my eldest brother, then a teacher, used to take us to a place outside the town and teach us how to use defensively the sticks *(lathi)* in the event of attack by policemen during *Satyagraha.* He himself joined the *Satyagraha* movement at Ankola in North Kannada district of British territory and started cutting palm trees from which country liquor, toddy, used to be extracted. The excise duty on 'toddy' was an important source of income to the British government. Another source was land revenue. As part of Civil Disobedience (*Satyagraha*) movement, the agriculturists were asked not to pay land tax. Serious attempts were made to cut off income to government from excise duties too. In the course of this *Satyagraha* movement, my brother Narayana was injured and hospitalised, but volunteers took good care of him. After some months, he came back to Shimoga.

THE ANATHALAYA

Anathalaya means in Kannada and Sanskrit "a shelter for the homeless" – crudely rendered in English as orphanage. It was in fact a home for poor students whose parents could not afford to meet the expenses on boarding and lodging. Some students had no parents. One social worker by the name Sri M. Venkata Krishnayya took pity on the poor students who were intelligent and eager to continue their studies in Mysore city because there was no college in any other town and not even a high school in smaller towns and villages of the state. He established the *Anathalaya* after much struggle where even today as many as 60 to 70 poor students are provided food and accommodation. Venkata Krishnayya, founder of this noble institution, was popularly known as the 'Grand Old Man' (*Vriddha Pitamaha*) and lovingly called *Tatayya* (grandpa). His life stands as a shining example of selfless service to humanity.

THE GRAND OLD MAN OF MYSORE

Venkata Krishnayya was given the title *Bhishmacharya* by Mahatma Gandhi for his determined efforts to help the needy and bring justice to the people. He was known to the public as one who laid the foundation of journalism in Mysore state and was called *Patrikodyama Pitamaha*.

Born in Maggem, a small village in Mysore, Venkata Krishnayya, son of Subbayya, had the benefit of learning Sanskrit, Telugu and Kannada languages and the ritual mantras befitting a Brahmin boy from his father. He used to listen to mythological stories recited by the great pandit Arunachala Sastry and was greatly influenced by the exemplary conduct of the heroes of the epics *Ramayana* and *Mahabharata.* After Subbayya's death, the family moved to Mysore. Venkata Krishnayya, too poor to study in schools, requested Bhagavata Subbayya to provide for his education which the latter readily did. Venkata Krishnayya passed the SSLC examination from Wesley Mission School. Although he could not go for higher education owing to poverty he was a good teacher, debater, intelligent and widely read. He could just maintain the family from the small fee he charged for teaching students privately and soon became renowned as a teacher in Marimallappa's high school. He was a great disciplinarian too. His great interest lay in educating the poor and mediocre students. When he found that many students without a home depended on weekly meals (meals provided by a family to a student on one day in a week), he established a boarding home for poor students. Initially, he himself used to collect small donations in kind and cash; later on, students had to collect them on Sundays from philanthropic families. Many lawyers and landlords were impressed by the efforts made by Tatayya and donated irrigated lands growing rice to the *Anathalaya*. This gift sustained the institution for nearly 40 years but unfortunately, the Mysore government passed a law transferring ownership of cultivable lands to tenants with the result that at one stroke this charitable institution which helped hundreds of students to educate themselves was deprived of the main source. The compensation provided by the government was just nominal. The institution suddenly found itself bereft of the means to feed hundred students daily. Gradually, it is now trying to collect donations from philanthropists to run the institution.

Venkata Krishnayya took up the cause of the poor and the helpless in the Legislative Assembly and became a secretary to the Standing Committee of the State Legislative Assembly. He entered the field of journalism and started the Kannada weeklies, *Vrittānta Chintāmani* (1885), *Sādhwi* and *Mysore Patrika* (1911) and an English periodical *Mysore Herald*. The credit for fighting for the freedom of the press in the early 20th century goes to Venkata Krishnayya. On his advice, Sir M. Visweswariah, Dewan of Mysore, gave greater freedom to the press. Tatayya was the founder of Saradavilas High School which was later on expanded into a college and technical institution.

2

College Days

My rustic language and dress brought comments from my colleagues in the Intermediate college which was an arts college. In 1936, the only college for science was situated in Bangalore. I preferred History, Economics and Logic for optionals and English and Sanskrit for first and second languages respectively. My first class in SSLC procured me a freeship which meant that I need not pay the tuition fee of Rs. 9 per month. I liked all the subjects because the lecturers taught in a simple language. The only problem I faced was with the lectures of Prof. A.B. McKintosh, a Scot who used to come to the class with his black gown on. For a student like me from a rural school, it was difficult to follow English with Scottish intonations. Luckily, I had nothing to worry because Prof. McKintosh took classes in English grammar and composition which my father had taught me very well. McKintosh was a nice gentleman and in fact so simple as to take everything a student said as literally true. One day a poor student told him that he depended on 'weekly meal.' The learned professor thought that the student had his meal only once a week. His compassion for the poor student must have melted his heart. Before the student could explain what weekly meal meant, the professor gave him a rupee or two and asked him to have a hearty meal in a hotel, which the student promptly did but later explained to him what the 'weekly meal' meant. McKintosh was still happy for having helped a poor boy. Another instance of McKintosh's misunderstanding the local English terminology was when the students of the college hostel wanted to have 'oil bath' in the 'festival of lamps' (*Deepavali*). He was astonished to learn that students take bath in oil instead of water, and thought each student may need a barrel of oil to bathe. He refused to allow this kind of nonsense in a hostel. The greatly disappointed students pleaded with Prof. C.R. Narasimha Sastry to convince McKintosh of the necessity of an 'oil bath' in Indian conditions. Prof. Sastry who was known for his humour was amused at the ignorance of McKintosh regarding the use of a small quantity of gingilee oil for massaging the body before a hot water bath. He agreed to speak to Prof. McKintosh and explained to him what the students meant by 'oil bath', whereupon the latter conceded the students' request.

I must say something about life in the boarding home *Anathalaya*, wherein about 45 students of the age 13-16 studying in various high schools, 5 in intermediate college, 10 in technical schools, 3 in BA or BT degree courses, and 4 in Sanskrit and Ayurvedic colleges lived. In addition to these regular boarders at least ten to twelve students were given 'weekly meals' in the *Anathalaya*. College students were wardens of 4 'blocks' consisting of 6 rooms each. In each room there used to be three students. All took cold water bath under the general tap, but I, because of my tonsillitis and frequent suffering from cold, had requested the cook Subbiah to provide me with hot water for bath, which he did. He was very strong, stout, strict and at the same time kind. Single-handed he used to cook rice and *dal* for 75 students at a stretch. In fact, he must have had superhuman power and divine grace to cook within two hours on firewood oven when there was no gas (he reminded us of Bhimasena as a cook in Viratnagara). Precisely at 9 a.m., the bell would ring and the hungry student battalion which had nothing to eat before 9 a.m. would move slowly in an orderly manner to the dining hall and answer the roll-call of the dining hall Warden K.V. Krishnappa, my great friend. He was a power to reckon with because he could report to the manager if anyone absented oneself without permission in writing. The late-comers were sent to the manager to be chided by him. The prayer sung in a chorus by 65-70 students was pleasing to the ear and soothing to the soul. It was in praise of God Siva *Samba Sadasiva sambho sankara saranam me tava caranayugam* was the first stanza. A couple of students who had classes later in the day would help Subbiah in serving food. After meal, students washed their dishes and rushed to various schools and colleges. I used to have a light breakfast at 6 a.m. in a small restaurant by way of a *dosa* for 3 *kāsu* (one *kāsu* was equal to 1/64th of a rupee) and a cup of coffee for 6 *kāsu.* At 9 a.m., I ate the meal in the *Anathalaya*. During lunch hour (1:30-2 p.m.) in the college I had a cup of coffee and in the evening a *dosa* in the University Health Kitchen, run by Mr. Rama Iyer, a kind Brahmin from Kerala. One can hardly believe now that for regular boarders, he would charge for a whole month providing two meals each day and a feast every Sunday only for 10 rupees. Food and all other daily needs were extremely cheap. Student life in the college and in the *Anathalaya* was really enjoyable. On *Ganesh Chaturthi* festival, all inmates of the *Anathalaya* used to enjoy a sumptous meal on the bank of Kukkanahalli tank. Some of the inmates of the *Anathalaya* attained high positions by sheer merit. One economist became the deputy governor of the Reserve Bank of India. Another, a law student, became a chief justice.

My friends in the college were H.V. Krishnaswamy Iyengar, Visweswara, B.H. Sridhara and Gopal Krishna Adiga. Among the inmates of the anathalaya, I could count only three, namely, K.V. Krishnappa, C.C. Subbaraya and K. Krishna Murthy as my close friends, who were always helpful. We used to play badminton in the anathalaya courtyard. I was given to reading history books loudly. In order to avoid inconvenience to other students in my block, Krishnappa, Subbaraya and I used to go to the Oriental Institute after dinner to read in the street light where the wind was cool and pleasant. After 10 p.m. we used to stroll on the banks of the large tank known as Karanji Kere. We could rest for a while on the wooden benches under the cool bowers. This tank had earned notoriety because occasionally a desperate student who failed in the Intermediate Examination used to commit suicide. As we had no such thoughts we could stroll without fear. Krishnappa, Subbaraya and I had formed a 'trio' – going together to the college, playing badminton and doing physical exercise. A separate hall was provided in the Anathalaya for physical exercise. We practised breath control, yoga *asanas* and *Suryanamaskara*. Like Ekalavya, we thought of our guru in absentia K.V. Iyer who had a separate gymnasium of his own in Mysore city.

Some of our idiosyncrasies had attracted the attention of our college mates. For instance, my friend Subbaraya considered a cat crossing his path as bad omen, and invariably either on our way to college or back, a cat, white or black, used to cross the road. Subbaraya who was always anticipating a cat in the side drain used to chase it away to prevent its crossing the road. We used to make fun of him as cat chasing Subbaraya (C.C. Subbaraya). Even if chasing the cat meant a few minutes delay in attending the class he did not mind it.

We planned excursions to places of historical importance such as Srirangapatnam, the ancient capital of Mysore kings where Tipu Sultan, son of Hyder Ali who had usurped the throne from Mysore Wodeyars, died fighting in the Mysore War fought with the British in 1799. We the trio along with five other students walked a distance of 10 miles and reached Srirangapatnam at 8 p.m. on a Sunday but we had no place to sleep at night nor any food to eat. Fortunately, the father of my classmate was the *Amildar* (head of the Taluk). My friend arranged a sumptuous meal for all of us and allowed us to sleep in the travellers bungalow. Next morning, we had *darsan* of God Ranganatha (Vishnu sleeping on the cosmic snake) in the famous temple, visited the beautiful Daria Daulat Palace of Tipu Sultan as well as the Gumbaz where his family members were interred.

The then ruler of Mysore State Krishna Raja Wodeyar and his successor Jaya Chamaraja Wodeyar were both great patrons of art and learning. During the former's reign the Oriental Institute was established. It is here that Dr. R. Shyama Sastry discovered the famous manuscript known as the *Arthasastra* of Kautilya, a guide book for rulers. It is a very ancient text (copy), more than 2000 years old, dealing with the administration of the state, the policy and principles to be followed by rulers and functions of the ministers, army generals and various departments of the government. Kautilya, also known as Chanakya, was unlike Machiavelli, an exponent of welfare state. After Shyama Sastry edited and published *Arthasastra* (text on Political Economy in Ancient India), his fame as a scholar spread far and wide. I mention here an incident which attests to his reputation.

When Krishna Raja Wodeyar was invited to attend the International Conference of Orientalists in Rome, it appears, he was introduced to the delegates as the Prince of Mysore state. One of the foreign delegates came forward and congratulated him as a prince 'coming from the land of Shyama Sastry'. Krishna Raja Wodeyar must have recalled the ancient adage in sanskrit *svadese pujyate raja, vidwan sarvatra pujyate* (the king is honoured in his own land but a scholar is honored everywhere); he sent a telegram to his officials in Mysore to give a promotion to Shyama Sastry. During this period, Prof. Asutosh Mukherjee, another famous scholar and vice chancellor of Calcutta University, requested the Maharaja of Mysore to lend the services of Shyama Sastry to the Calcutta University. The Maharaja did not want the state to lose his services and therefore made Shyama Sastry the Director of the Oriental Institute. Subsequently, Prof. Mukherjee invited Shyama Sastry to deliver a series of lectures on *Arthasastra* and honoured him by giving him Rs. 5000. Shyama Sastry told me this story in 1938 when I, as secretary of the University History Association, approached him to inaugurate the Association.

The senior intermediate examination was the toughest. However, I could pass it in 1938, obtaining a high II class and standing second in rank for the entire state. That year, none passed in Arts in I class. One can imagine how difficult it was to obtain 60 per cent marks in those days. It is because of this high rank, I was awarded Merit (subject) scholarship of Rs. 15 per month in addition to exemption from payment of tuition fee of Rs. 15 per month in B.A. Honours course. As I had obtained 80 per cent marks in Economics as well as History, I was given a seat in both courses, but I preferred History to Economics because my father advised me that a study of Indian history and culture would help appreciate the art, religion and philosophy of our own country. Later,

I felt that my father was my greatest guru who knew by intuition my natural inclination for art and culture. In fact he had laid the foundation for it by teaching me Sanskrit language and taking me on a tour to visit ancient temples and festivals.

The Bachelor of Arts (honours) in History was a 3-year degree course with eight major papers, namely, Indian History and Culture (Ancient and Modern), History of Europe, Economics (Principles), Political Science, British Constitutional History, Modern Industry and Recent Economic History of India. There were 6 minor subjects: English Literature, Sanskrit, Archaeology, Economics, History of Great Britain/History of Civilisation and a special subject (Hoysalas). The course gave wide scope for a student to understand and appreciate the political and economic history and recent trends in India, Great Britain and the world as a whole. For the first two years I continued to stay in the Anathalaya but in the third year I had to leave the institution as I was to get married. I rented a room for Rs. 2 per month in the same building where Prof. Srikantha Sastry also lived on D. Subbaiya Road very near to Maharaja's College. In the first year (1938), Subba Rao and I went to Shimoga during the Christmas Holidays and from there to Jog Falls, the highest waterfall in India.

ADVENTURE IN JOG FALLS

My friend Subbaraya and I planned a visit to Jog Falls, the famous waterfall (Fig. 2). The River Sharavati which takes its rise in the Western Ghats in Karnataka state, meanders through lush green tropical forests of tall teak, sandalwood and other commercially valuable trees, after cutting into the granite hill, takes a sudden leap from the precipice of the Western Ghats to a depth of 900 ft. Fed by monsoon rains from May to August, the river cascades down to the plain.

The four cascades are named Raja, Rani, Roarer, and Rocket. The vertical face of the rocks overgrown with shrubs all around the Falls is hidden by the mist rising from the river bed at the bottom of the fall. In 1938 the engineers were just planning to harness the waterfall for producing electricity after building a dam and installing suitable turbines, etc. under a scheme prepared by the renowned engineer-administrator, Sir M. Visweswariah of Mysore. My friend and I quickly gulped a cup of coffee in a small restaurant at Sagar railway station and got some quantity of *Kesaribhat* (a sweet preparation of wheat) packed in plantain leaf and jumped into a government-operated bus which led us through narrow winding roads negotiating the thickly wooded hill slopes descending from 2000 feet to 1000 feet. By the time we reached the plateau at Jog village we were turned into the Reddleman of Thomas Hardy's novel, *The Return of the Native*. Other passengers including a few school urchins and boisterous youth started rushing to an improvised reed-hut from the eve of which hung a board announcing its name in English 'Vasant Bhavan', where they expected a good hearty breakfast of hot *idlis* and *dosas*. They were disappointed. All they could get was a cup of bitter coffee with hardly any milk or sugar – both were scarce in this apology for a restaurant. I inquired from a local villager whether it is possible to go down the valley to reach the bottom of the fall. He said, "Yes. There are steps." Without a second thought, at 10 a.m. we started climbing down the hill barefooted but carefully keeping our feet on the slippery, uneven stone steps. After going down a hundred steps, we found that there were only boulders rendered more slippery by the overgrowth of lichen and moss. Already wet and shivering, we had to crawl on the boulders, sometimes losing our grip. As we went further down, thorny shrubs on either side slowed down our speed. We had left our packet of food midway in the hope of eating it on the return journey. After a last minute desperate crawling we reached the bottom of the cavern at 3 p.m. Though exhausted and hungry we had the satisfaction of touching the bottom of the waterfall. Pausing for a while to enjoy the grand scenery of the waterfalls, chirping of birds amidst swaying branches of smaller trees above, we felt as if we were embraced by nature itself. It was getting dark and we were completely drenched by the splashing cascades of water. Without further hesitation we started climbing up the hill opposite the waterfall where the massive boulders looked like sculptures in the midst of shrubs. Further above, the trees were swinging their arms as the wind blew. We were in too great a hurry to stop and admire this beauty. To our horror we found that we had missed the original route we had climbed down. It was already dark and under precariously held grips we had to negotiate the vertical face of the rock. Sometimes I used to lie down on the top of a boulder and extend a hand to Subbaraya to enable him to come up. At others, he would go a few steps above and lend me a helping hand. As we were just about to reach the summit of the cavern we heard the cries of jackals, which instilled more fear. At one stage both of us secretly thought that we were lost forever. But by God's grace we could negotiate the slippery and jungle-covered rocks and reach the edge of the plateau. It was already 8 p.m. and completely dark without any trace of human activity in the neighbourhood. We had come to an entirely strange spot where there was no shelter. Bewildered by the ghastly situation, I climbed a tree to see if I could spot a village light. Some distance not very far away, I could see some dim light. We decided to go in that direction. After brushing aside some shrubs we could trace a footpath which when carefully followed led us to a small village of 8 or 10 huts. But as soon as we approached the village dogs started barking and some villagers came running with long sticks thinking that robbers had come. When we shouted in a shrill voice that we had missed the way and wanted some help, they lifted their lanterns and held them to our face. Perhaps they could read helplessness and innocence on our faces and after initial inquiries allowed us to enter the village. One couple, about 60 year old, offered food when we told them we were very hungry. The lady of the house offered a cake made of *ragi* (millet) and a cup of buttermilk; we slept in the hut for the night. Next morning the villagers showed the way to the nearest bus station. The rattling bus came two hours late bringing with it a cloud of dust but giving us enough time to have a breakfast with hot coffee in the restaurant.We were given back seats wherefrom we were thrown down at every bump on the road. At last we reached Shimoga in the evening. This unanticipated adventure and our daring efforts to climb the heavily-wooded hills at night gave us the confidence to face any danger in wilderness. It is this experience that emboldened me to undertake many risky jobs on land and in the sea in the course of my long service in the Archaeological Survey and National Institute of Oceanography.

In the first year of my B.A. honours class in Maharaja's College there were only four students including me. H.V. Krishnaswamy Iyengar who was smart and intelligent, but as poor as I, was my close friend. Sitaram Mudaliar, another classmate, was certainly an earnest student and was better placed financially. S. Krishnamurthy was irregular in attendance. We were very fortunate in having M.H. Krishna, a renowned archaeologist, as our professor. He had a doctorate from the University of London, and worked under Sir Flinders Petrie. Professor Krishna, who was simultaneously the director of archaeology, had conducted excavations independently at the ancient site of Brahmagiri where there is an inscription of the Mauryan Emperor Asoka recording on the rock the tenets of Buddhism and instructions to the officers of the state for serving the people. Chandravalli was another early historic site which was carefully excavated by him. Prof. Krishna was a great patriot who discarded the Western dress and wore *dhoti*, a close collared coat and a turban. His profound knowledge of Indian culture was astonishing. When he lectured to B.A. students on Indian culture, everyone listened with rapt attention. The Prince of Mysore (later Maharaja) Jaya Chamaraja Wodeyar, a student in B.A. class, attended his lectures. Prof Krishna instilled in us the spirit of social service and motivated us to fight for the freedom of India. Once, all students of Maharaja's College and intermediate college joined the general strike organised by a national leader. J.C. Rollo, an Englishman, who was the principal came down from his chamber in the first floor and asked us to attend classes, which we refused to do. He warned us that those who had the benefit of scholarship would be deprived of it. I was one among them. Next day I told Prof. Krishna about the threat; he asked me to continue the strike, and if need be, he would make good the monetary loss. This is an example of his patriotic fervour.

MARRIAGE

On a Sunday in March 1940, an old man, a devout Madhwa Brahmin met me in the *Anathalaya* and raised the topic of my marriage with his grand-daughter. I rather reluctantly agreed to see the girl in his house in Saraswatipuram extension. The girl was good looking and after her father offered me a cup of coffee, she was asked to sing a song. In those days, a girl had to be well versed in classical music (Karnataka), and the would-be bridegroom's parents or bridegroom himself would ask if she knew vocal or instrumental music. The girl sang in melodious voice, a devotional Kannada song on Krishna *(Krishna ni begane baro)* the divine lover of young maids (*gopis*). I was glad that she knew music and told her parents that I had to consult my parents. In reply to my letter, my father wrote back that her horoscope did not match with mine. So I had to drop the idea of marrying that girl. The next girl that I saw was the daughter of an officer in the Bangalore Secretariat. I did not feel that she was a suitable bride for me. A month later, I received a telegram from my father saying that I should meet him immediately at Shimoga. I took the next available train and reached the place the following morning. It is then that my mother with a smile on her face, told me that she and my father had seen a nice girl for my marriage and her horoscope matches well. I was asked to see her before giving my consent. Hurriedly, I went with my parents to the residence of Karanji Krishna Rao, the respected businessman in the town. I had heard of him as an honest wholesale merchant of grocery. His daughter, Kamala fair and well-built came to the hall where we had assembled. She also sang in a sonorous voice two songs, one each on Krishna composed by Saint Purandaradasa of Karnataka and another by Tyagaraja, both exponents of Karnatak music. Moved by Kamala's melodious voice and her devotion to God I gave my consent for the marriage. It was fixed in the month of *Ashadha* on *Sukla Navami* in July 1940.

The next eventful day was the convocation of Mysore University in 1941 when the degree of B.A. Hons. was conferred on me and the Sir Hugh Candy Gold Medal for first rank was also awarded. My parents and wife witnessed the award ceremony. The next day we went to see the famous Brindavan Gardens and the illumination of fountains and flower beds on the bank of River Kaveri, against which the Krishnaraja Sagara dam is built. The other two attractions during Dussehra festival are the temple of Ranganatha as Seshasayi Vishnu at Srirangapatna and the illumination of the Mysore Palace noted for its unique architecture.

During my final year of B.A. Hon. course, my friend Krishnaswamy used to come to my room for joint study. Although we were competitors in the class for subject scholarship which is awarded to the student getting highest mark, we exchanged notes without reservation. Krishnaswamy used to write small handbills for advertising the movies. With him, I saw several English and Hindi movies. Among the English ones, I liked the film *Marie Antionette, Hunchback of Notre Dame de Paris*, etc. Among Hindi films produced by New Theatres, the *Kapala Kundala* adopted from Bankim Chandra Chatterjee's novel and *Dharati Mata* appealed to me most. More than the movies I enjoyed dramas by famous actors Varadachari, Hiriyanna and Sabu. Most of the dramas were mythological.

A BRAVE GIRL LOCKS UP A TIGER

After I passed B.A. Hon. (three-years degree course) with credit, standing first in first class for which I won the Sir Hugh Candy Gold Medal, I continued my studies in M.A. class for about six months and then joined the postal department as I was in need of a job. As a trainee at Honnali and as a temporary hand in Shimoga post office I learned the working of all branches. But my father did not like my continuing in a department where there was no opportunity for either teaching or research. From Shimoga I was transferred to Sorab. Next to the post office lived Ranganatha Rao Kale, a pharmacist dispensing allopathic and ayurvedic medicines prescribed by the local allopathic doctor (licensed medical practitioner). Mr. Pundit Ranganatha Rao's brother Parasuran Kale lived in a house on the outskirts of Sorab town beyond the River Varada. There was heavy jungle growth all around Kale's house. One day Parasuram Kale's daughter Leela who was alone in the house went into the dark cattle shed adjoining the house at about 10 o'clock in the morning. She saw a tiger sleeping inside! Scared by its presence, but without making any noise, she came out. With a unique presence of mind she closed the door and bolted it. She ran upstairs of the main house and started shouting from the window overlooking the main road "Tiger is in, call *Appa* (father)." A stranger walking down the road, who responded to her call for help, was told that the tiger is in the cattle shed, and he should not open the door. The stranger went to Kale Ranganatha Rao's shop and related what the young girl had told him. Ranganatha Rao and many others rushed to the house and on examination from the roof of the country-tiled cattle shed, they were convinced of the tiger's presence. Among the crowd that had gathered outside the shed, one lean and hungry looking man Giriyappa, the local hotel keeper, opened the door slightly and peeped in. The tiger rushed out, hitting him in the face with its claws. He was severely wounded and admitted to the local hospital. The tiger which jumped out of the cattle shed got stuck up in a thick bush. It is then that the forest officer decided to shoot it. It was killed and taken in a procession on a bullock cart. Cheered by urchins, the 'brave' forest officer led the procession in the main streets of the town.

During my tenure in Sorab I suffered from typhoid. The fever did not subside after 21 days. I was weak and worried. That night I had a dream in which Saint Raghavendra Swamy assured me of recovery and desired that I should do *seva* in the *Matha* at Shimoga. After reaching Shimoga, I fulfilled my vow.

I passed my M.A. examination from Nagpur University and obtained the degree, I joined the *Nagpur Times*, an English daily in 1946 owned by the then Chief Minister of Central Provinces (later Madhya Pradesh), Ravishankar Shukla, a renowned freedom fighter. This paper was sustaining steady losses and I realized the folly of joining a press that could not pay its staff promptly. Before resigning I attended an interview for the post of assistant director of archaeology in Baroda. After the interview I went back to Nagpur and completely forgot about the interview. While at Shimoga, I received a letter on 1st March 1948 that unless I join the post of Assistant Director on or before 5th March 1948, the Baroda government order will be cancelled. Hurriedly, I reached Baroda on the 5th and joined the post. Thus, I entered the field of archaeology for the first time and felt that my father's wish was fulfilled by God's grace. He was happy to see that his son had an opportunity, though in a distant place, to study ancient monuments and inscriptions and to participate in the preservation of the cultural heritage of India. In this job my knowledge of Sanskrit and Hindi was very helpful.

3

An Archaeologist in the Making

I had the privilege of learning important branches of archaeology such as epigraphy and numismatics under a sound scholar Anant Shankar Gadre, director of archaeology at Baroda. My college study in archaeology, in general, was also helpful. Gadre had a well-planned two-year training programme for me. I was to be trained in exploration of prehistoric sites, in scientific excavations, and conservation of monuments and excavated sites under eminent archaeologists. At the engineering school (Kalabhavana) in Baroda, a special program for training me in architectural drawing, surveying and photography was also on the anvil. Dr. Herman Goetz, the German scholar who was the director of the Baroda museum and also the art gallery (*Kirti Mandir*), taught me museum methods.

TRAINING IN PREHISTORIC ARCHAEOLOGY

The Fifth Gujarat Prehistoric Expedition under the guidance of Prof. Dr. F.E. Zeuner of London University Institute of

Archaeology and Prof. H.D. Sankalia of the Deccan College and Research Institute, Poona were to survey the Sabarmati, Mahi and Narmada valleys in December 1948. Before surveying the valleys of the Sabarmati and Mahi rivers, the expedition party had to visit the excavation of a microlithic site at Langhnaj, undertaken by the Deccan College, Poona and the Boroda State Archaeological Department. I was deputed to join the excavation at Langhnaj, a small village in Meshana district of north Gujarat. The objective of the excavation was to ascertain the cultural horizon of the microlithic tools of chalcedony, mostly of geometric and non-geometric shapes found scattered here. The age and environmental conditions of the times when these microliths set in bone or wooden frame to form sickles and harpoons were used, had to be determined. The tools were triangular, trapezoid or lunate in shape and a few had a sharp point. They were produced on thin flakes of siliceous material. The depression between the dunes once served as tanks where water used to collect in wetter conditions. In the absence of human skeletal remains it was difficult to identify the people living under such conditions and practising hunting, fishing and perhaps cattle-rearing also. In the earlier excavations, a few animal bones, including those of rhinoceros, were found, which indicated that at one time the climate must have been wetter. The occurrence of hand-made pottery was another problem for the archaeologist. The excavator, B. Subba Rao has tried to identify two cultural periods at Langhnaj – the first one yielding animal and human bones and the second, hand-made pottery along with stone tools in both the periods. Stone maceheads have also been found in Period II. A similar repertoire of cultural artefacts without any Neolithic element was found by me at Rangpur in 1953-54. The absence of neolithic axes in the subsequent period has created a gap between the Late Stone Age and Neolithic Period in Gujarat.

To resume the story of the prehistoric expedition in 1948, the truck in which the camp equipment was loaded broke down on the way 3 km from Langhnaj. This forced us to camp on the open railway platform of a small station at Garinja for the night. The party consisted of Dr. Sankalia and his wife, Dr. Iravati Karve, Dr. Zeuner, S.B. Deo, M.N. Deshpande, K.V. Soundara Rajan, Sheik, Isaac, M. Seshadri, and myself. Mrs. Karve and Sankalia prepared *kitchdi* (rice and dal) which we ate late at night and slept on the platform. The villagers had warned us that there may be dacoits in the neighbourhood. This kept us awake especially when we heard some shouting. In the meanwhile, Mr. Gadre brought a relief vehicle and took us to a nearby rest house. The same night, it appears, the dacoits had attacked a village and we felt lucky to have escaped their attention.

EARLY STONE AGE IN INDIA

Indian pre-history began with the discovery of the first palaeolith by the British Geologist Bruce Foote at Pallavaram near Madras. To understand the problem of Indian pre-history, it is necessary to understand the progress made in the subject. The prehistoric settlements of the Indian subcontinent belong to a stage when man, as a food gatherer and hunter, was wandering in the forests more than one million years ago. Elsewhere in Africa and Java, his existence goes back at least to two million years when he used chipped stone as tools to dig up roots and scrape the hides of animals which he killed. The human remains and stone tools are termed as belonging to Old Stone Age (Palaeolithic stage) of the Pleistocene Period. Geologically, our glacial periods and three interglacials are recognised during the long history of man's existence. As there is hardly any human fossil left in the Siwalik Hills of Punjab in the North and in the Narmada Valley in the South, the prehistorian has to depend on stone tools left by man which lie in gravel beds of rivers and their feeders. A few animal fossils have been found in the Siwalik Hills and Kashmir as well as Narmada and Godavari beds. Recently, a fragment of a human skull of Palaeolithic Age was reported from the Narmada Valley.

The prehistorian in India is trying to correlate the Indian Old Stone Age industries to those of the primary division of techniques of tool-making in Africa and Southeast Asia. Two broad divisions of tools, namely, core and flake tools have been recognised. In the former case, the core is chipped so as to obtain a suitable cutting edge while in the latter case the tool is made of a large flake and worked into a hand-axe or scraper or cleaver. There is also a third group known as chopper-chopping industry in India. So far as climatic phases are concerned, the pluvial conditions of India are correlated to the glacial conditions of Europe. The North Indian stone industry is a flake industry and that of South India is a core-flake industry. Rough flake tools belonging to the second inter-glacial are found in Potwar in the northwest and in Upper Narmada at Hoshangabad. Perhaps these tools belong to the terminal phase of Lower Pleistocene contemporary with the Pithecanthropoids of Java. Leaving for the present the Early Soan Industry of Kashmir belonging to Middle Pleistocene, we may confine ourselves to the core-tool industry of Lower Palaeolithic of Central and Western India which is also known as the Madras-Acheul Industry. A few tools of this industry found in Soan Valley Interglacial Phase have helped to place the tools of Madras Industry found in Pluvial Period. The Madras tools are pear-shaped, mostly flaked on faces. Some oval-shaped ones have a cutting edge all around. The core tools are profuse in the south and flake tools in Central India. The Madras industry, said to have been the result of hammer-stone technique, is similar to the Chelles-Acheul industry of France. No clear picture of the life of Lower

Palaeolithic man using such tools can be had in India. He must be of nomadic group using stone axes, scrapers, etc. The Uranium-Thorium dates for Acheulian tools of Krishna basin are 200,000 yrs BP. Only one fossil of an archaic *Homo sapiens* has been found in India, but not of any *pre-erectus.* While Central and Southeast Asia claim a long chronology, India cannot. The next phase known as the Upper Palaeolithic and noted for blade tools was widespread in France and other European countries. But it is hardly traceable in India. The recent discovery of a few metal harpoons of 2nd millennium BC found in copper hoard sites are presumed to be copies of barbed bone or antler points of upper Paleolithic industry. According to D.H. Gordon, the Central Indian rock shelters of Hoshangabad and Bhimbhetka where there are rock paintings are not of Upper Paleolithic Period. He assigned them to 5th century BC. But it is necessary to emphasise here that the Mesolithic (Middle Stone Age) industry of coarse blades, points, and burins of siliceous material found in some of the rock shelters of Itar Pahar, in Madhya Pradesh can be associated with the rock paintings (IAR, 1959-60).

The Acheulian industry of India is dominated by hand axes and cleaver, with a significant proportion of bifaces. This is especially thc case in the river-beds of Betwa and Gambhiri. In the Pedhamli-Hirpura sectors of the Sabarmati Basin, hand-axes are more in number. A few core tools are also present. In Saurashtra, a Middle Paleolithic Phase noted for the fine grained, siliceous material used for scrapers has been identified by Sankalia and others. Finally comes the Late Stone Age – Microlithic industry of Langhnaj. Perhaps it was succeeded by the Neolithic Phase when man became a full-fledged food producer and settled down in villages.

I participated in the survey of the Sabarmati bed and its banks at Pedhamli and Virpura. Here, Zeuner explained to me the formation and exposures of laterite of great

Fig. 3. Author's family, Lower row (L to R): Meena (daughter-in-law), Gopal (son), Upper row (L to R): Upendra (grandson), Kamala (author's wife), author and Nandini (grand-daughter).

thickness overlying the basal beds of sandstone and shale. Over the laterite the thick-cemented gravel, reddish silt and yellowish sand could be seen. The laterite of the banks belongs to the penultimate glaciation. When we reached the Loharnala of Pedhamli, we could identify a factory site of tools, mostly cores with pebble surface with one or two large flakes removed. This implementferous gravel belongs to the last interglacial. In northern Gujarat there was a long dry phase, but with sufficient precipitation and a cover of dry forest or scrub. Later, during my exploration in Saurashtra it was found that Rojdi, a Harappan site, rests on a silt deposit on Bhadar bank. Below it is a fine gravel overlying a pebble bed resting on rock almost similar to the section in Rangpur.

My wife Kamala came with our newborn child, Shakuntala from Shimoga to Baroda in July 1950. We rented a small house for Rs. 25 a month in Sayajiganj, a good locality in Baroda city. This city was known as the cultural centre of Gujarat. A new university was just then established encompassing several institutions such as the Oriental Institute, Kalabhavan (engineering college), Medical College and College of Education which were already well-known. Dr. B. Subbarao was appointed lecturer in archaeology in the department of history and culture. I was given training in architecture drawing, surveying and museum methods in the departments of engineering and museums.

AMRELI EXCAVATION

Dr. Subbarao wanted to excavate the early historic site of Amreli to ascertain its precise cultural sequence based on stratigraphic evidence which was lacking in the earlier excavation undertaken by Dr. Hirananda Sastry and A.S. Gadre. The rich collection of coins and other antiquities from Amreli lying in the Baroda museum had to be classified and catalogued for the report. Dr. Herman Goetz, director of the museum, not only extended facilities for me to classify the antiquities but also gave useful direction for preparing the report. In the meanwhile, at the instance of Dr. Subbarao, Dr. Jivaraj Mehta wrote to the director-general of ASI stating that the university would like to excavate Amreli. Mr. Gadre was upset because it was he who had excavated the site earlier. I read his mind and politely suggested that in view of my experience and training in excavation, I can as well undertake excavation at Amreli to which he readily agreed and gave what little money was left in the year's budget to start the excavation. With only Rs. 250, I proceeded with a draftsman, D.H. Shah and a photographer, Bhagavath to Amreli.

In the course of excavation, I came across hitherto unknown features of Amreli, which was a Gupta-Kshatrapa settlement. An important feature brought to light was the practice of post-cremation burials with megalithic features. The second feature was a large brick structure of Kshatrapa period which could be identified as a Buddha *vihara*. The antiquities found are an inscription reading *Isvarasya* and several terracotta Bodhisattva figures (for details see *Excavations at Amreli*). Among the earlier finds, mention may be made of the stone plaques of Vishnu and Mahishmardini and a stone mould of a goldsmith depicting flying figures of Greco-Roman features. A unique feature of pottery found at Amreli is a large polished ceramic bowl of almost paper-thin walls fired in inverted firing technique. It was highly polished. On the basis of a distinct ware known as Red Polished Ware, we could determine the cultural sequence of Amreli and fix the date of occupation between 1st century BC and 5th century AD.

A. Ghosh, Joint Director-General of ASI, who visited the excavation at Amreli, was pleased with the results and agreed to augment the staff of the excavation section. He appointed K.M. Srivastava as technical assistant. Ghosh and I visited a site known as Veni Vadar near Amreli where he identified the protohistoric pottery of the site as analogous to the Sothi ware of Bikaner in Rajasthan which he was exploring during those days. I casually mentioned to him that Subbarao had complained that the director-general's office had not sent a reply to Jivaraj Mehta's letter. He smiled and said, "It is sometimes convenient not to reply to such letters." His remarks indicated that ASI had presented the Amreli excavation as a *fait accompli*. Ghosh's visit infused confidence in me to undertake exploration and excavation independently.

MY MOTHER

My mother, a devout Vaishnavite, was anxious to visit the holy place Dwarka after staying for a week with my sister Sita in Bombay. When she came to Baroda, she was upset regarding my sister's illness and the loss of a holy *Varaha Tanki* (a gold medallion of Vijayanagar depicting the coronation of Lord Rama) which she worshipped daily. She used to eat food cooked only by her with the result that she did not get much rest. One day she complained of headache and arthritic pain. I took her to Dr. Pathak who on examination found her having very high blood pressure and wondered how she was surviving. He advised bed rest for her but she would not take sufficient rest. It so happened that when I was at Pratapnagar Railway Station at Baroda in September 1950, I got a message that she suffered a stroke. I rushed back and got her examined by the specialist, Dr. Prahladbhai. He administered some medicine and warned that if she gets another attack she might not survive. After a week she showed some improvement, but all of a sudden she had another stroke and collapsed. On receiving the sad news, my three brothers, came from Bangalore, and her obsequies were performed at Ankleswar on the bank of holy Narmada. I felt sad that I could not take my mother to Dwarka for the *darśan* of Lord Krishna. However, her second annual ceremony was performed by me at Dwarka. After a few days, we shifted to a more spacious apartment in the first floor of Parasuram bungalow. My first daughter Shakuntala, quite mischievous and intelligent, could learn dancing in a couple of months time from a Bengali dance teacher, Mr. Das. Subsequently, she was trained under a professional dancer Kalyanraman and his wife Sita, both artists of the Baroda palace. Shakuntala gave a public performance of Bharatanatyam dance at the age of seven (June 1955) during the anniversary of the Kannadasangha at Baroda. This function was presided over by Nittoor Srinivasa Rao, former chief justice of Karnataka High Court. It may be interesting to note that 30 years later, Shakuntala's two daughters, Charumati and Sowmya, who had learnt Bharatanatyam in Madras gave a public performance in 1978 at Bangalore, which was again presided over by Srinivasa Rao. The renowned artist, S. Roerich, his wife

Devikarani, former minister of education, V.K.R.V. Rao and others congratulated the young artists.

Owing to my transfer to Nagpur, Agra and other places, Shakuntala, Gopal and Nalini had to study in different schools in various states which indirectly helped them to learn Hindi, Gujarati, Marathi and Tamil languages in addition to English and Kannada.

EXCAVATION OF SAHASRALINGA TALAV

In the winter and summer months of 1949-1950, I continued excavation of an eleventh century lake known as Sahasralinga Talav constructed by the Solanki ruler of Gujarat Siddharaj at Patan in Mahesana district of Gujarat. The Solankis belonged to the Chalukyan dynasty of Karnataka. The ruler had brought some earth workers known as *Veddas* from Karnataka. Among the labourers was a beautiful girl known as Jasma whom Siddharaj wanted to marry but she refused. After finding no way to escape from Siddharaj's advances, she is said to have committed suicide. There is a ballad on this episode – *Jasma Ode* – which is popular even now in Gujarat. The tradition says that as a result of her curse the tank went dry, perhaps because it was a year of drought. Some astrologers are said to have advised the king that if human sacrifice is offered, there will be rain to fill the tank. A Harijan offered to sacrifice his life provided the king removed some of the disabilities of the Harijan community. The king agreed and the Harijan sacrificed his life. How far this story is reliable is not known but the fact remains that the removal of the disabilities of the Harijan communities is recorded. The *Saraswati Purana*, a medieval Sanskrit text, says that Siddharaj got the lake excavated not only to supply water to the capital Patan but also to serve as an irrigation tank. He further ensured regular supply of water from the nearby Saraswati River by excavating a canal through which water flowed into the silt chamber (*Rudrakupa*) where silt got deposited and clean water flowed into the lake through three circular rock-cut outlets (*Triveni*) which were decorated with sculptures of Brahma, Vishnu and Maheswara. Further, all along the bank, 1008 small shrines with *linga* installed in them were built and connected by a chain passing through the pinnacle so that when the queen pulled the chain the bells in all the shrines rang. This fact is mentioned in the *Saraswati Purana*. In order to verify this statement, excavation was conducted that led to the exposing of several small shrines. The engineering skill exhibited by the builders of the lake is remarkable for the age. Near the Rudrakupa there is an apron wall to arrest scoring effect of the water flow into the tank. At the other end there is a wasteweir. This was exposed by me and got examined by an expert engineer, Mr. Chapekar, formerly of the famous Sakkur Barrage (now in Pakistan). He agreed that the fly levels indicate that the tank was designed suitably to allow water from the river into the basin and excess water to escape through the wasteweir.

EXCAVATION AT RANGPUR

Sometimes, discoveries by chance are of such great importance that archaeologists are drawn to them again and again. One such discovery was made in 1934 in a small sleepy village known as Rangpur on the River Bhadar in Limbdi Taluk of Surendranagar district of Gujarat. While cutting across the ancient mound for laying out an approach road to the village, large quantities of pottery and some terracotta objects were found and sent to M.S. Vats, then superintendent of the Archaeological Survey of western India at Poona. Mr. Madho Sarup Vats, who had attained great fame by his excavation at Harappa in Punjab, excavated Rangpur and came to the conclusion that it was an outpost of the Indus Valley Civilisation (ASIAR, 1937).

It was hard to believe that Indus people could have made a settlement so far south of the Indus Valley. Later, G.S. Ghurye of the University of Bombay dug up the site once again and agreed with Vats' conclusion. But not satisfied with the earlier findings, Mr. M.G. Dixit and Dr. H.D. Sankalia of the Deccan College Poona undertook excavation of Rangpur in 1947. They expressed doubt about Rangpur being an outpost of the Indus civilisation. This controversy assumed great importance after the partition of India as there was no site of Indus civilisation left within the present day borders of India. In one of the meetings of the Central Advisory Board of Archaeology held at Delhi, a member historian asked why the ASI was unable to make any headway in finding sites of the Indus civilisation east or south of the Indus Valley. In fact, he asked whether ASI had only dwarfs. As an observer at the meeting, I felt that it was a challenge which should be accepted and planned survey should be undertaken in Rajasthan and Gujarat. Amalananda Ghosh, then joint director-general, undertook survey of the dried-up bed of the ancient Saraswati River (Ghaggar) in Bikaner division of Rajasthan and discovered a few sites of painted pottery resembling Harappan ware but he designated the culture as Sothi culture which is now found to be a pre-Harappan culture. He asked Subbarao at Ahmedabad whether he would like to excavate Rangpur but he declined. Subsequently, Ghosh made the offer to me and I readily agreed for two reasons; first, I was glad that Ghosh could entrust such a crucial site to me and second, I thought it would give me a unique opportunity to excavate an Indus civilisation site of such importance as Rangpur. I surveyed the site in 1953 and found that earlier excavators had concentrated mainly on the central part of the mound. I preferred the slope behind the village where I found some Harappan pottery and baked bricks exposed in a rain gully. I laid the trenches here and exposed right from the top mud brick walls and burnt brick drains built on large terrace-like platforms of mud bricks (For details see *Ancient India*, 18-19; *Excavations at Rangpur and other explorations in Gujarat*, 1963, p. 2-207, ASI). A very brief account of the cultural sequence and major finds is given here. Three cultural periods are distinguished in Rangpur: Period I (the earliest) is noted for a Late Stone Age Culture where microliths and a few Series II tools of siliceous materials were in use. Period II is subdivided into IIA (Harappa Culture), IIB (Late Harappa Culture) and IIC (Transition Phase of Harappa Culture). Period III (Post-Harappa Culture) is noted for a distinct pottery designated as Lustrous Red Ware which was evolved from the Harappan shapes but in a degenerate fabric. In Period IIA, Rangpur was a small town depending mainly on agriculture, growing rice and millets. A terracotta figure of a horse found here suggests that the people knew the animal. The town had certain civic amenities such as underground and surface drains built on mud-brick platforms to avoid destruction by flood. Four structural phases in Period IIA are noticed here (Fig. 4). Each one was destroyed by flood in the River Bhadar which was flowing nearby. The houses had two or three rooms and the residents were fairly well-off as can be inferred from the presence of beads of gold, steatite, carnelian, shell and terracotta. Among the tools, the typical Harappan copper celts have been found. Triangular terracotta cakes used for ritualistic purpose were recovered from fire altars. Pottery of sturdy red and buff fabric had shapes identical to those of Indus civilisation. The more prominent types are perforated cylindrical jar, basin, dish-on-stand and S-shaped jar. But, the goblet and beaker are extremely rare. A local ware known as the Micaceous Red Ware was also in use and its typical shape is a bowl with a small stud handle. In Period IIB deurbanisation is indicated by poorly built houses and lack of some of the typical

Fig. 4. Four structural phases of Period A, Rangpur.

Harappan tools and ornaments. During this period the township shifted to the central part of the mound and the overall decoration of the pottery was lacking. Civic amenities hardly existed. At the end of Period IIB an accelerated change in the overall cultural equipment is a striking feature. Here the term 'deurbanisation of the Indus civilisation' is used for the transition phase of the culture by some archaeologists. It needs some clarification. Deurbanisation is often taken to mean the total reversal of forces operating in the urban phase. True, Rangpur was now less populated, trade diminished, and fewer industries are noticed. But it must be remembered that the people did not sink into complete backwardness nor were they illiterate. The stone weights confirm that the trade was still going on. After the initial decline, a slower rate of growth is witnessed in Rangpur in Period IIC which is termed as the Transition Phase, when the village came to be expanded and signs of recovery in trade became visible. There was considerable modification in the shape of vessels. For example, the convex-sided bowl became concavo-convex. The dish had a rounded edge. Another feature of Period IIC was the introduction of a new technique of wet-smoothing the vessel surface which gave it a shining red colour. This ware is christened Lustrous Red Ware. It is also decorated with black horizontal and wavy lines and motifs of stylised peacock on a lustrous red surface. Period III witnessed prosperity. The township extended in area and the houses had larger rooms. The builder used potsherds in the foundation of houses to serve as a waterproofing course. The long chert blades of Period I were replaced by short blades of chalcedony. The Lustrous Red Ware and the Black and Red Ware were in great use. There was a Coarse Red Ware in which jars with high neck and round base were prominent. A chalice or wine cup was another type in use.

The excavation at Rangpur opened a new chapter in the history of Indus civilisation by adducing evidence of its decline, transformation, and survival in Gujarat during the four centuries following the end of the prosperous cities of Harappa and Mohenjodaro. Rangpur is an index site for tracing the evolution of Harappa culture. The results of the first year (1953) excavation published by Ghosh in IAR 1953-54 had raised a volley of questions in the Central Advisory Board of Archaeology regarding the identification of Rangpur as a Harappa culture settlement which Sankalia had questioned owing to the absence of the typical Indus seal. For three days, I had to answer several questions in the course of which all details of the finds and the evolution of the culture were traced. In order to confirm our findings it was decided to excavate Rangpur once again. This was a challenge which I accepted. In order to convert a challenge into an opportunity I suggested that if a better site is found in the course of my proposed exploration of Saurashtra to trace the route taken by the Harappans, I would prefer it for excavation.

4

Discovery of Lothal

As a sequel to the symposium in the Central Advisory Board of Archaeology, it was found necessary to ascertain whether Rangpur was only a backwash of the Indus civilisation. I therefore took up exploration of the estuary of the rivers Bhogavo and Sabarmati near Rangpur, since the Indus civilisation was considered then a riverine civilisation. Our survey party which included the technical assistant, K.M. Srivastava, conservator Sheikh and photographer N.C. Shah, started exploring the ancient mounds near Dholka on November 13, 1954. But we found no Harappan site. On the contrary, our jeep got stuck up in the mire near Arnej. Here there are no roads and the flat low-lying area is flooded during monsoon. We were told that November was not a suitable month for jeep journey. We thought of going back to Baroda but halted for the night in the temple at Arnej. Next morning we could get a cup of tea and no breakfast. After offering prayer to the Goddess Arnejmata, we started looking for ancient mounds. As we proceeded towards Lakshmipura we could see in the horizon a mound

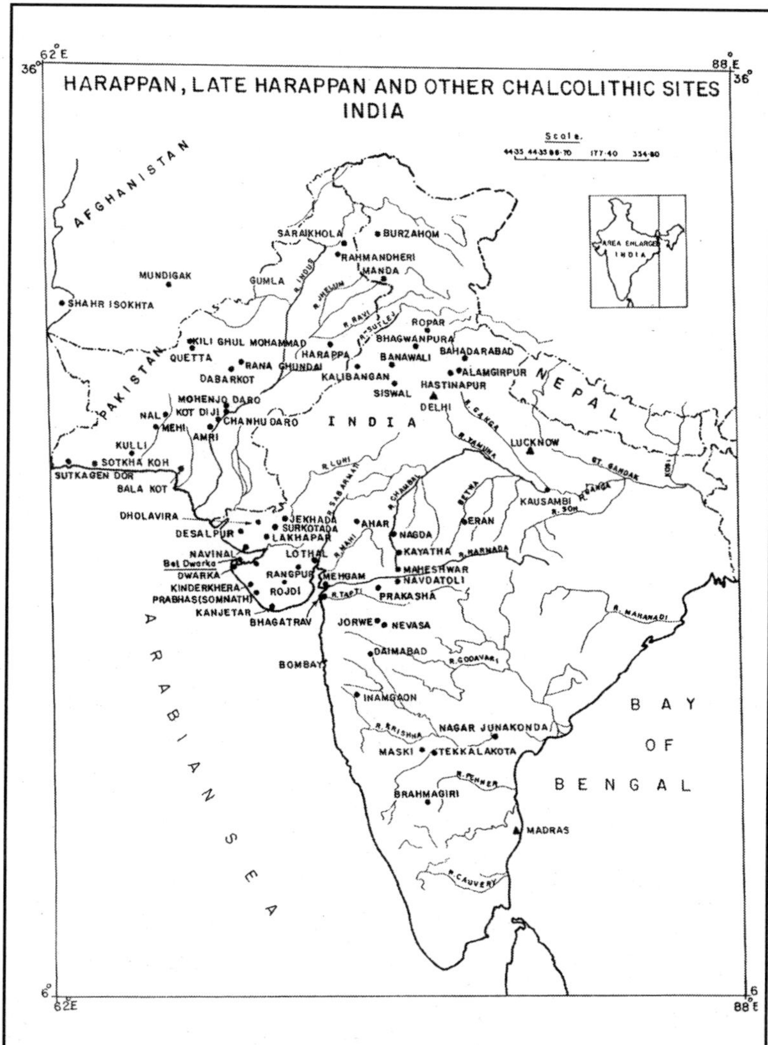

Fig. 5. (Map) Harappa, Late Harappa and other chalcolithic sites, India.

protruding from the flat water-logged surroundings. We suspected it to be an ancient site but that was only our wish. After driving a short distance, we came across a marriage party of colourfully clad ladies and men led by Mr. Mehpat Singh. I asked Singh whether the mound sighted by us yields any potsherds of the kind which we showed him. Normally during exploration, we carry some samples of pottery for villagers to understand what we were in search of. Singh told us that the mound is strewn with this kind of pottery. As the owner of the land, he volunteered to take us to the mound now known as Lothal, provided we could wade through knee-deep water and slush, which we did without hesitation. After a brisk survey, we could recognise the pottery of mature Harappa culture lying on the surface. Our joy had no bounds and we collected not only potsherds but also other artefacts, such as long chert blades, faience beads and terracotta cakes, all characteristic of mature Harappa culture. The previous day we had noticed similar sturdy red pottery at the site known as Koth but we were not sure about its association with Harappa culture. After scrutinising pottery from Lothal we were confident that the pottery from Koth also belonged to Harappa culture. Discovery of Lothal confirmed my belief that if one's intention is good and sincere efforts are made, one is sure to reach the goal.

MORE HARAPPAN SITES

After rejoicing over the discovery of the Lothal mound we undertook further exploration towards the corridor of Wadhwan in north Gujarat in order to trace the probable route taken by Harappans to reach Saurashtra. We were successful in locating a number of small Harappan sites known as Pansina, Babarkot, Akru and Devaliyo – all situated within a radius of 10 km from Rangpur. Further north, within Ahmedabad district, we located a post-

Harappan site at Kanasutaria. This site was exposed to view as a result of a bulldozer cutting across the mound while laying out a road by the Public Works Department. The importance of the site lies in the fact that it provides a clue to the climatic changes during, before, and after Harappa culture. The mound overlies a microlithic cultural deposit under which lie a fine gravel bed, and further below it is a coarse gravel deposit of the river. Overlying the microlithic deposit is a post-Harappan settlement which in turn underlies aeolian deposit of recent times. The site was excavated later and it was found that there is a gap between microlithic and post-Harappan settlements. As we went further north towards Kutch, we could locate some Harappan sites belonging to different phases. Among them is Desalpur, a mature Harappan site which was partly eroded by the river. It may be recalled here that Rangpur was also eroded heavily by the River Bhadar. Obviously, most of the Harappan and late-Harappan sites in Saurashtra and partly in Kutch and north Gujarat were subject to heavy flood and consequent erosion of the settlements. The more significant among the Harappan sites in Kutch are Khirasar, Navinal, and Todio. Kinderkheda and Kalianpur near Porbandar and Gop and Narmana in Saurashtra and Sujanipur in Mahesana district in north Gujarat have been plotted for their relative importance in various phases of Harappa culture.

P.P. Pandya of the Saurashtra State Archaeology Dept. was a very enthusiastic explorer. He undertook exploration all by himself and discovered as many as 50 sites of the Harappa culture belonging to various phases among which the more important ones are Pabumath, Surkotada, and Dholavira. He added at least 50 sites more to the list of Indus Valley sites in Gujarat and excavated quite a few of them, including Prabhaspatan, Rojdi and Pabumath. Special mention of Pandya's efforts has been made here because he was anxious to conduct a village to village survey even without caring for his health. This ultimately led to his sad demise. It was a great loss to archaeology.

EXCAVATION AT LOTHAL

The ancient mound presently known as Lothal (74 degrees, 14 minutes, 25 seconds East, 22 degrees, 31 min., 23 sec. North) is now easily approachable by road from Ahmedabad which is at a distance of 85 km. The railway station nearest to Lothal is now known as Lothal-Bhurkhi on Ahmedabad-Bhavanagar section of the western railway. The word Lothal in Gujurati language conveys the sense "mound (*sthal*) of the dead (*Loth*)," same as Mohenjodaro in Sindhi language. The ancient township and dockyard are now preserved for visitors to see. There is also a site museum where antiquities and models are exhibited.

In February 1955, when excavations were started at Lothal, we had to face many problems. There was no road from Ahmedabad or from the nearest town Dholka, 30 km away. For daily provisions for the camp, one had to go to Dholka and for specific requirements to Ahmedabad, which was the only major city where we could get tools needed for digging. The excavation lasted for nearly 7 years and each year we were working for 8-9 months at a stretch from October to June. Sometimes the temperature used to cross 110 degrees Fahrenheit. We pitched a large number of tents to accommodate the staff, trainees, and equipment. The photographer had to improvise a dark room for developing the negatives immediately after photographs were taken in the early morning or late in the evening. Ghosh was kind enough to see that technicians from headquarters were sent to Lothal periodically. I had to conduct a school of Field Archaeology in which as many as 20 scholars from different universities, museums and archaeological departments were undergoing training.

Amalananda Ghosh, director-general, like a true scholar, gave all possible help to conduct the excavations and conservation. He posted Dr. Sunil Ray, a sound scholar, as deputy superintendent to attend to routine work. Ghosh was himself a very able administrator and appreciated good work. One day in Lothal camp he found a marksman greatly devoted to work and wanted that I should promote him which I did.

Dr. Paramasivan, chief chemist, sent Mathur to set up a laboratory for chemical treatment of excavated finds. Gupta was our anthropologist who exposed and studied on spot the human skeletal remains. Dr. Bhola Nath of the Anthropological Survey of India took all animal remains to Calcutta for study and report. Athavle, a geophysicist, took samples of the (burnt) clay from the warehouse blocks. Joseph, Saxena, Vyas, Mukherji and Kantilal Tripathi were among other technicians at site.

It was my good fortune that I had very competent draughtsmen, surveyors and photographers in Joseph, Natvarlal Shah, Mathadhikari, L.K. Jain and Mohinder Singh. Charcoal samples were collected and sent to the Tata Institute of Fundamental Research Bombay for C 14 dating. The reputed industrialists of Ahmedabad, Chinubhai Seth, Ambalal Sarabhai and Scientist Vikram Sarabhai, chairman, Atomic Energy Commission, his wife Mrinalini, a renowned dancer, and many others took keen interest in our excavation. Vikram got the impressions of cloth on the terracotta sealings examined by experts in the Ahmedabad Textile Research Institute and the Physical Research Laboratory. Professor Ms. Priyabala Shah took to field-work in all seriousness.

We had pitched up ten large and five small tents in addition to *shamianas* for holding exhibitions and for kitchen, dining hall, stores, etc. The photographer got a large pit dug in the ground and covered it with tarpaulins to serve as dark room. The labourers from Rangpur and other villages had built about 25 huts for themselves. In summer we used to live in reed-built huts which were much cooler than tents.

Originally the Lothal mound must have been much larger. It is now dwarfed by silt deposit at the foot of the mound. Ravages of nature and vandalism have resulted in the destruction of the brick structures. The excavation was begun in the central part of the mound and trenches were extended on grid-iron plan to obtain cross sections at close intervals in cardinal directions.

Lothal town, though smaller in size than Harappa and Mohenjodaro, is an example of perfect Harappan town planning (Fig. 6). It follows the dichotomy of dividing the town into Acropolis corresponding (Fig. 7) to the Citadel and the Lower Town. In addition, there is the unique tidal dock on its eastern flank. The cemetery lay in the north-west corner outside the peripheral mud-brick wall which enclosed the Acropolis and the Lower Town, the latter noted for a Bazaar street (Fig. 7). Within the Acropolis where the ruler lived, the houses were built in a row each having a brick-paved bath connected to public underground sewage through a tunnel with an inspection chamber for removing solid waste (Fig. 8). The Acropolis was strategically located to enable the ruler to keep a watch on the movement of ships in the dock and the transaction of goods in the warehouse. The Lower Town, occupying a major part of the town, was divided into six blocks on which houses stood in neatly planned groups on artificial terraces of bricks. The purpose of building houses on 1 to 3 m high platforms was to keep them above the normal flood levels.

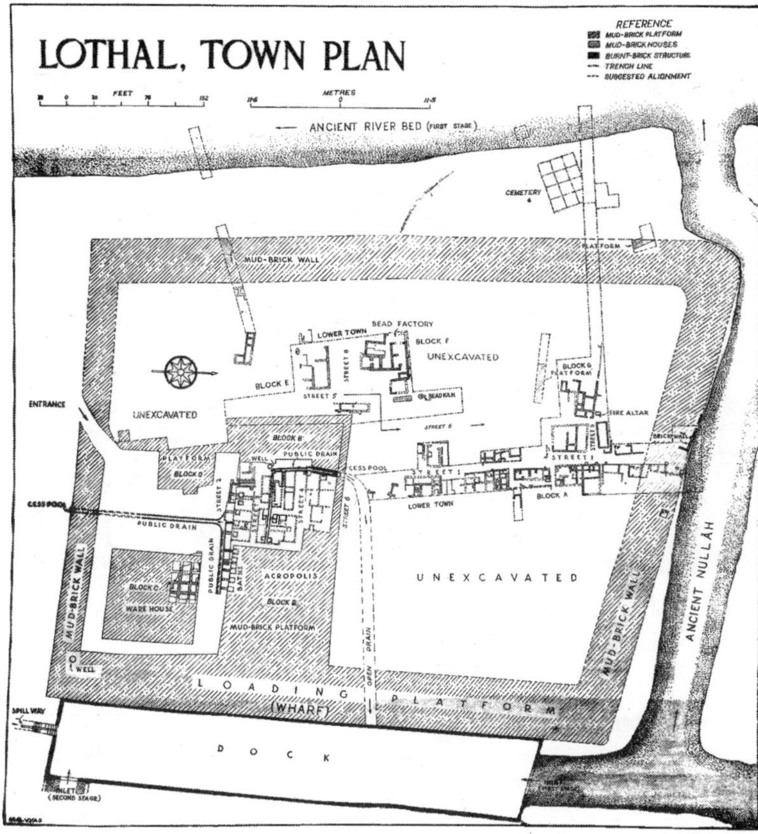

Fig. 6. Lothal – town plan.

Foreign Trade

The economy of Lothal depended more on trade than on agriculture which supplied rice, wheat and barley to sustain the craftsmen. In a merchant's house, Indus seals, gold jewellery and imported pottery have been found. Bead-making was the second major industry which brought enough wealth through export trade. A large factory where lapidaries worked together and were provided with living quarters has been laid bare in the industrial sector. In the nearby double-chambered furnace raw material, namely,

Fig. 7. The Bazaar Street in Lower Town, Lothal.

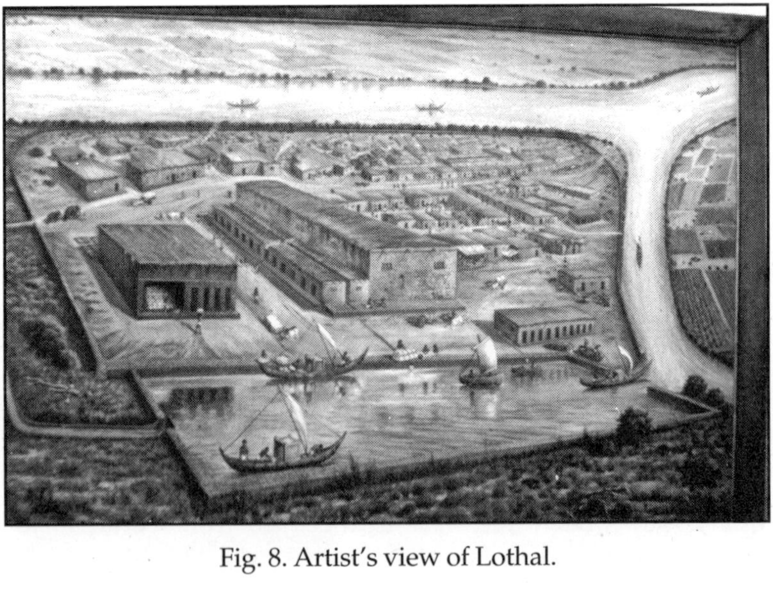

Fig. 8. Artist's view of Lothal.

pebbles of agate and chert as well as finished beads were heated in earthen bowls filled with sawdust. The present day lapidaries of nearby Cambay town follow the same technique. Several cylindrical and barrel-shaped beads of Lothal origin are found in Asmar, Kish and Ur in Western Asia. The technique of etching is said to have travelled from India to West Asia just as the technique of Reserved Slip Ware of pottery travelled from West Asia to cities of Indus civilisation. Apart from beads, copper ingots seem to be another commodity exported from Lothal. The reference in the clay tablets of Ur to import of copper ingot and the discovery of a Bahrain type seal in Lothal and Indus seals, weights and pottery in the tombs of Bahrain indicate brisk overseas trade of Lothal. The reference to a dock (in Nippur tablets) in the land known as 'Dilmun' (Paradise of Sumerians) is best attested by the unique dockyard laid bare at Lothal. Here elephants were known, which is again a feature of Dilmun. S.N. Kramer is of the view that Lothal was 'Dilmun', the paradise of Sumerians, where according to their epic, "The sun rises first and the cities are clean."

DOCKYARD

One of the major contributions of the marine engineers of Lothal is the construction of the earliest tidal dock of the world in 2300 BC (calibrated 2500 BC). By selecting a site for the artificial dock on the eastern margin of the town, they avoided siltation of the basin by the river and danger to the ships while in the main current. The basin walled by kiln-fired bricks, which were too precious to be used even for building houses of merchants, measures 219 m north-south and 38 m east-west. This dock is larger than the modern Bombay Merewether and Visakhapatnam docks. The inner face of the brick walls of Lothal dock is in perfect plumb to enable boats to berth touching the edge of the wharf (Fig. 9). The inlet in the northern embankment was wide enough to allow easy entry for ships in low tide, while the lock-gate system of the outlet in the southern embankment ensured a minimum draught of 1 to 1.5 m in ebb tide. According to oceanographers Panikkar and Srinivasan, the Lothal dock being a purely tidal one, the Lothal engineers must have possessed adequate knowledge of tidal effects,

Fig. 9. The eastern brick embankment wall of the dock, Lothal.

the amplitude, erosion and thrust. From this knowledge they developed competence at Lothal for receiving shipping.

This is perhaps the earliest example of knowledge of tidal phenomenon being used practically. In 1986 Rajiv Nigam, a scientist from NIO, Goa collected samples from 1 m depth of the floor of the dock and analysed them. The analysis shows profuse presence of gypsum and the micro-organisms *foraminifera* indicating that the tidal sea water used to enter the basin, which conclusively proves the basin to be a dock.

The Sea Goddess

I told Ghosh during one of his visits to Lothal that I intended excavating the sout-heast corner of the mound, where I expected some salient as in Mohenjodaro. Narayan, an intelligent labourer from Gundi, asked me not to disturb the stones symbolising the goddess Vāṇuvatimātā housed there and worshipped by local people, but I ignored his suggestion and started excavation here. First, we noticed chunks of burnt mud plaster with impressions of reeds which indicated that the structure had a wooden roof covered with mud plaster and reeds. As we dug a few inches deeper, 12 blocks of mud bricks, each 3.6 m square and 1 m high, with intersecting passages between them came to light. These passages were paved with kiln-fired bricks. Originally there were 64 blocks, standing on a massive mud brick platform, which were destroyed in due course by flood waters. In some passages terracotta sealings with clear impressions of seals on one surface and of packing material on the other were found.

In addition to excavation at Lothal, I had to look after conservation of monuments at Chittorgarh in Rajasthan. Here I received a telegram from Srivastav saying that in an accident a labourer had died on Lothal site and a few others injured were admitted in the hospital at Dholka.

I immediately left Chittorgarh and travelled by jeep day and night covering about 1000 km and reached Lothal. The injured were taken care of. But the other labourers refused to go back to work, and attributed the accident to the wrath of Goddess Vāṇuvatimātā. In spite of my efforts to convince them that the accident was not due to the wrath of the Goddess, they continued their strike for more than a week. An idea came to my mind whereupon I asked Kantilal Tripathi, the marksman, to get up at night and announce that the Goddess had asked him to summon Rao Saheb (as I was known to workers) and declare that the Goddess is not displeased with our work. He added that I should build a shrine for her at a place about 200 m away from the mound as desired by the devotees. I agreed to the suggestion and next morning excavations were resumed on the mound of the warehouse and the foundation was laid for the temple at the pre-determined site. This incident shows how strong the feelings of the local people were about their sea goddess. Subsequently, the dockyard discovered in excavation near the warehouse mound confirmed that Lothal was a port perhaps presided over by the Goddess of the sea. According to a folk song, she came to Lothal from Sind via Rann of Kutch and went southward to Hajira near Surat. Her full name is Vāṇuvatī Sikotarīmātā. The Survey of India topographic map mentions a Sikotarimata near the Rann, again one each at Hathab (Gogha near Bhavanagar) and Hajira near Surat. All the three places are Harappan sites.

The warehouse of 64 blocks criss-crossed by air vents and passages was built close to the dock. Goods were inspected, sealed and stored here (Fig. 10). The commercial use of Indus seals is confirmed at Lothal where 70 impressions on clay labels (sealings) affixed to packages have been preserved. The impressions of packing material of cargo are of bamboo mats, reeds and chords tied to packages.

Fig. 10. Indus seal (Lothal) with a motif of mountain goat, fire altar and inscription.

Seals and Indus Script (Fig. 11A-B)

Lothal has yielded 150 seals and 70 sealings, the former mostly made of steatite and faience. All of them, chronologically arranged on the basis of stratigraphic evidence, indicate an evolution of the Indus script from a partly pictorial and partly cursive writing into a purely cursive writing in the late phase. The pictures of hill, pipal leaf, scorpion, etc. noticed in early seal inscriptions are omitted in the later ones. This important feature of simplification of writing which was limited to 22 basic signs is corroborated by the evolution of writing noticed on the seals at Kalibangan, Dholavira and Banawali and in late levels of Harappa and Mohenjodaro excavated by G.F. Dales. The pictures of pipal leaf, scorpion, etc. had ceased to have picture value, as can be made out from the addition of cursive signs to these pictures. Sometimes joining of the

Fig. 11. Indus seal impressions (sealings), Lothal, no. 1 inscription on one side and cloth impression on reverse.

cross sign with the hill sign and field sign with cursive sign can be seen in the inscriptions.

The structural analysis of Indus signs shows that there were only 64 basic signs including pictures in the early phase which were later reduced to 22 + 2 = 24 cursive signs (for details see Rao, S.R., 2004). The adding of short strokes to basic cursive signs for indicating their vowel value and the joining of two or more basic cursive signs for forming conjunct consonants or syllables (such as *pta, pat, pr, papr,* etc.) are features which were continued in Brahmi script of 3rd century BC in India. The process of identification of basic signs can be followed in Figs. 13A-B.

The phonetic value of 17 out of 22 basic cursive Indus signs was determined on the basis of the phonetic value of

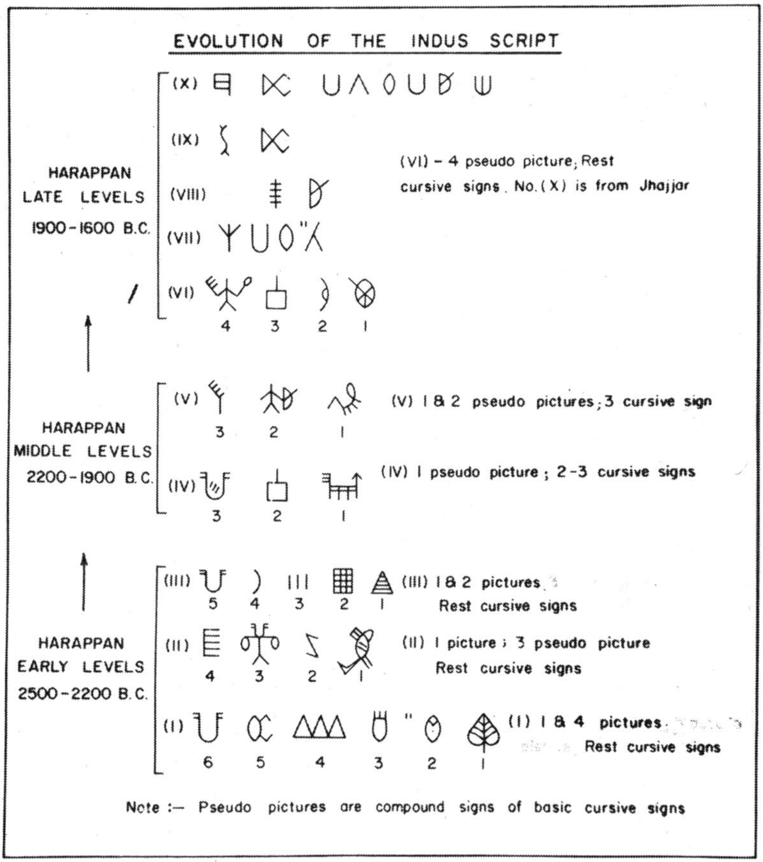

Fig. 12. Evolution of the Indus script.

identical signs of the already known Semitic script (Fig. 14). The words *aeka (aika), hapta, daśa, śata,* for 1, 7, 10 and 100 in Indus inscriptions are also in Indo-Aryan/Iranian language. Other cognates, *śāsa* (ruler), *pat* (protector), *bhaga* (lord), *maha* (great), etc. – occurring in Indus inscriptions indicated Indus language to be related to Old Indo-Aryan (OIA). In the first stage, about 50 cursive inscriptions with signs analogous to the Semitic signs but having vowel indicators were read and the language was identified as OIA. In the next stage the signs of man and fish were given

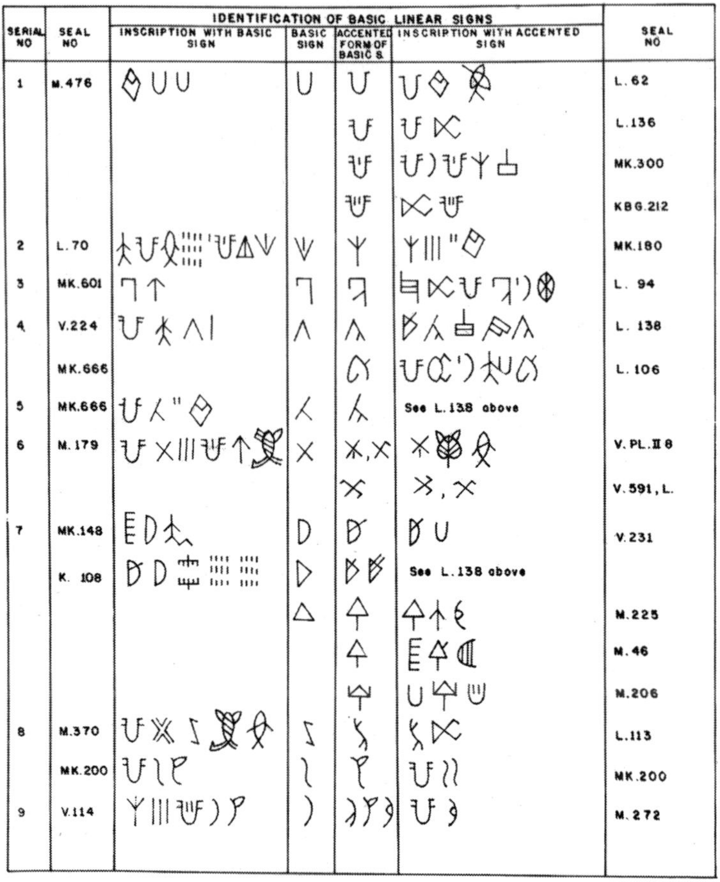

Fig. 13a. Identification of basic cursive (linear) signs.

phonetic value and respectively, which enabled me to read 200 inscriptions which confirmed that Indus language was related to OIA. Finally pictures of hill, field and pipal leaf were given single sound or syllabic value on acrophonic principle from OIA words. For example, *śak* from *śakuna*, *aśv* from *aśvattha*, *vṛṣ* from *vṛścika* for bird, pipal leaf and scorpion are words traceable in Vedic and Avestan texts (Fig. 15). The methodology of decipherment, the vocabulary, semantics, syntax and other grammatical features common

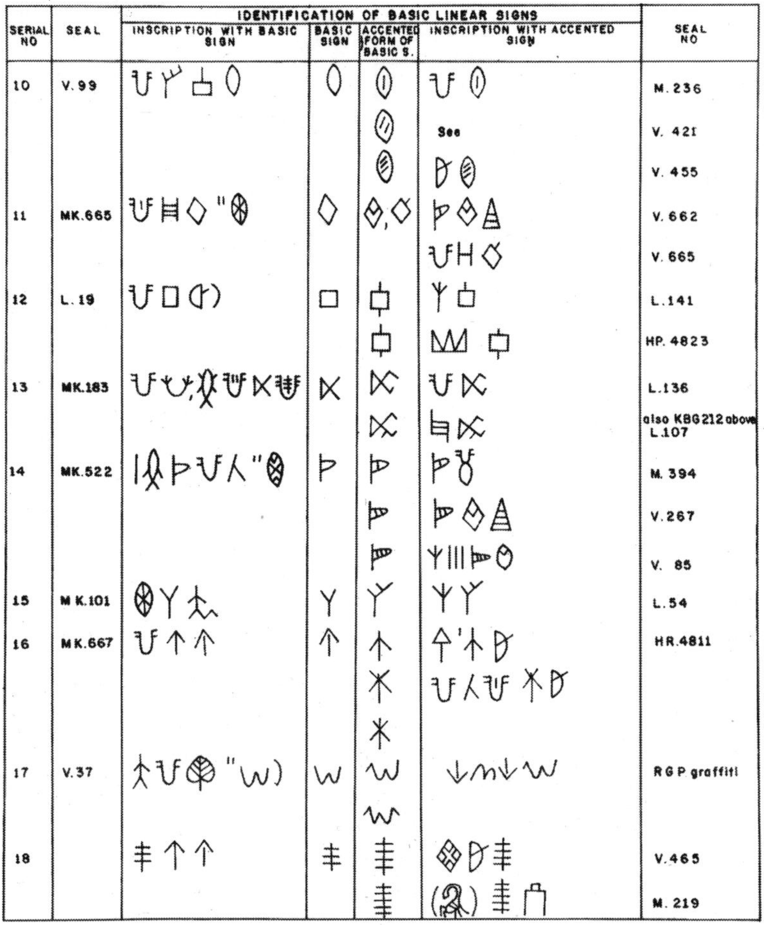

Fig. 13b. Identification of basic cursive (linear) signs.

to OIA-IIR and Indus are referred to in the *Alphabet Gallery* (2004). The seal inscriptions furnish valuable information on the rituals, cosmic origin, hierarchy of rulers of different regions of the Indus empire and the fire cult as well (Fig. 16A-B). The Harappans at Lothal were fire worshippers and also performed animal sacrifices. Two types of brick altars built for fire-worship have been found in the excavation. Some residents venerated the animal also. In

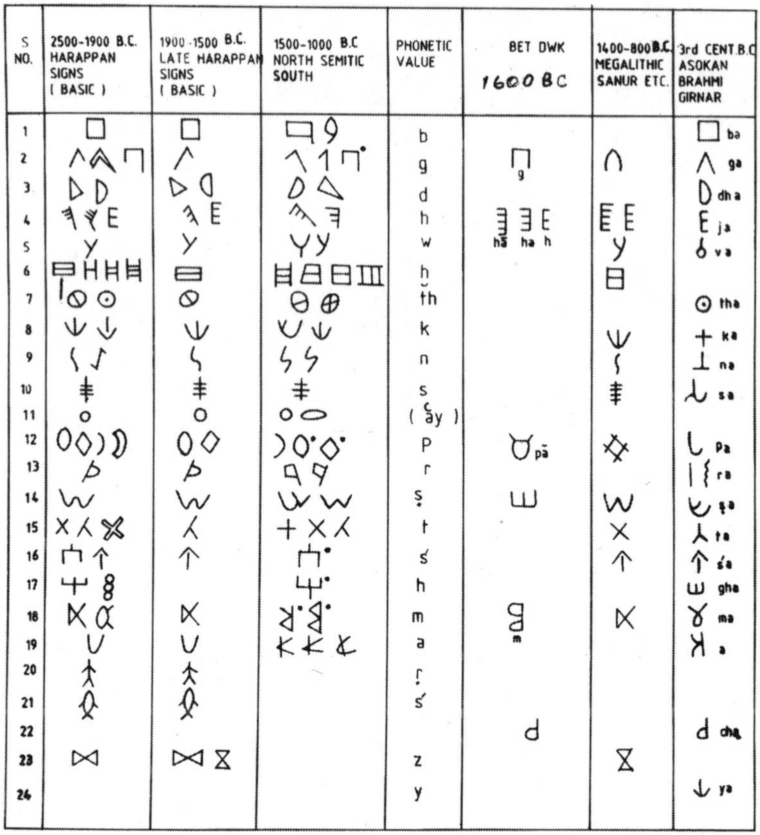

Fig. 14. Phonetic value of basic Indus, Semitic and Brahmi alphabetic signs.

the sacrificial altar at Lothal, a gold pendant similar to the *Rukma* mentioned in the *Rigveda* and shown on the forehead of the statue of the priest from Mohenjodaro was found. The so-called brazier on Indus seals with unicorn motif resembles Persian fire-altar. Vedic type of fire-altars are rectangular, semi-circular or circular. Another type (apsidal) has a brick stele in the centre. The tricephalic God seated in yogic posture and surrounded by animals is Agni who was also known as Paśupati (Lord of Animals) in *Śatapatha Brāhmana* (Fig. 17).

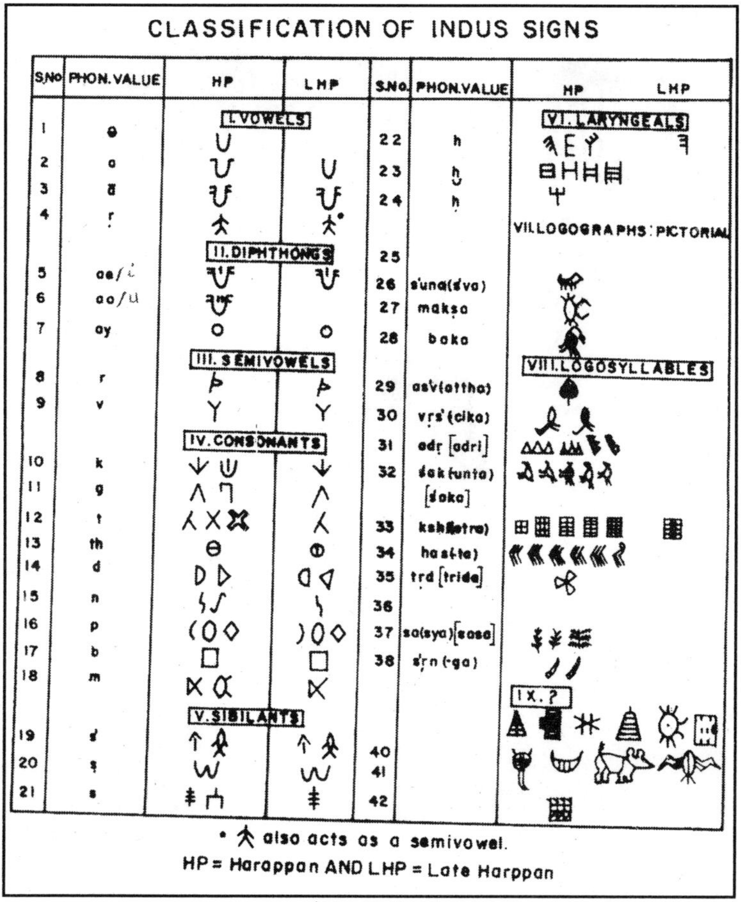

Fig. 15. Classification of Indus signs.

Professor V. Gordon Childe visited Lothal excavations (Fig. 18) and I availed of the opportunity to discuss with him the use of seals and sealings and the anti-flood device of peripheral walls at Lothal. He congratulated me on discovering and excavating Lothal.

Arts and Crafts

The Lothal jewellers produced fine jewellery using microbeads of gold and steatite (Fig. 18). Gold pendants

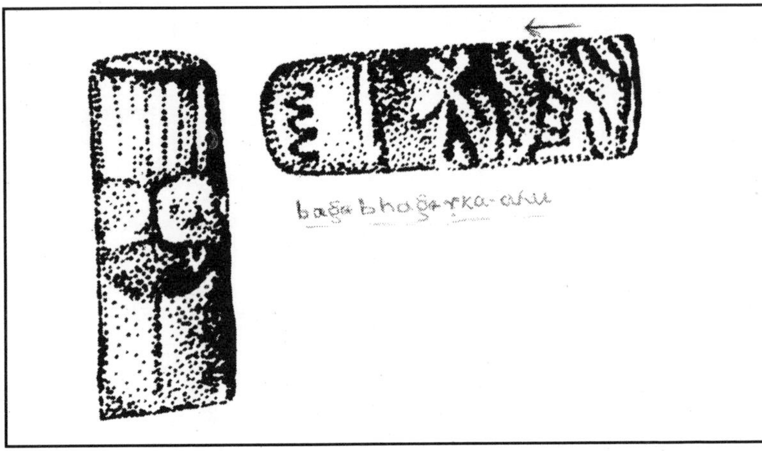

Fig. 16a. Fire-altar motif with inscription reading *baga-bhaga-rka-ahu* (Harappa).

Fig. 16b. Fire God (Agni) in anthropomorphic form standing in an arch of flame. Inscription reads *bhaga-rka* (Harappa).

Fig. 17. Three-headed Paśupati (Agni) surrounded by animals.

and rings have also been found here. Bead making was a major industry of Lothal. Raw materials such as carnelian, agate and jasper brought from Bhagatrav in south Gujarat were processed here into attractive beads and exported to Bahrain, Oman, Sumer and Afghanistan. Gold used in Lothal came from Kolar and Hatti mines of Karnataka (Rao S.R. 1991).

The coppersmiths of Lothal produced copper of 99.84 per cent purity, free from impurities such as arsenic, while the copper ingots of Harappa and Mohenjodaro contain arsenic and other impurities. Perhaps it is the purest copper ingot of Lothal which was in demand abroad and is mentioned in Nippur clay tablets. Low-tin and high-tin

Fig. 18. Gordon V. Childe visits Lothal.

bronze was used by Lothal smiths to produce animal figures, tools, weapons and ornaments of copper and bronze. The reference to *guburam* in Sumerian clay tablets was perhaps to Lothal copper ingots. The clay tablets of Ur refer to Dilmun as the 'Paradise of Sumerians'. Kramer is of the view that Lothal and other Indus cities constituted 'Dilmun' since the reference to dock, elephants and clean cities could only be to Lothal and other Indus sites.

The homogenity of industrial products was ensured by the Harappans by standardising the form and content of goods. Ornaments, weapons and sophisticated tools such as the circular saw and twisted drillbit of bronze were all produced to a uniform standard. Artefacts produced from imported raw materials were available even in small villages. Goods had to be sealed for authentication by the state authority after the cargo was examined in the warehouse. It may be of interest to note that Harappans put their technological knowledge to peaceful use and not for producing weapons of war.

Weights and measures were standardised for facilitating domestic and international trade. Cubical weights of chert and agate were in decimal and binary system. For weighing goods the lower weight was of 27.584 gm and the higher one of 546.07 gm. The lower Indus weight is related to the English ounce and to the Greek *uncia* of 27.21 gm. Perhaps the latter was modelled on the Harappan unit of 26.611 gm. Lothal has yielded a series of gold discs in decimal graduation beginning from 50 mg in the ratio of 1, 2, 3, 4, 6, 8, 20, 25, 30 up to 3250 mg. They were used for weighing precious objects like pearls, gold and silver or served as currency. The 100 mg unit corresponds to the weight of the *gunja* and the 50 mg weight to *dhānya,* or half *gunja* of the *Arthasastra,* a 3rd century BC text.

Agriculture was well developed. Wheat, barley and rice were in use at Kalibangan. A terracotta sealing from

Lothal has the motif of a seed-drill. The average length between two divisions on the ivory scale of Lothal is 1.704 mm. The 6th and 21st divisions are marked by longer lines indicating a decimal graduation. Ten divisions of Lothal scale are equal to one *angula* of the *Arthasastra.*

Lothal suffered from abnormal floods in 2300 BC, and again in 2200 and 1900 BC. After the first two floods the town was rebuilt. The major flood in 1900 BC destroyed the dock, forcing the residents to migrate to safer places. The few who returned were poor and lived in jerry-built houses until 1600 BC. During this phase, the Lothal village lacked civic amenities. Trade declined and the craftsmen migrated to other regions.

As the c 14 date for Lothal Phase III B of Period A is calibrated to 2708 ± 135 BC (Sonwane 2002) @5730 half life; the earlier Phases I and II of Period A should be dated 2800 BC. Earlier, I had dated Lothal Phase I to 2500 BC (uncalibrated).

The Lothal folk enjoyed a few indoor games like chess and dice. For chess they had shell, terracotta and ivory chessmen. One full set of chess gamesmen in terracotta found at Lothal is similar to the set found in the tomb of Queen Hatshepsut in Egypt. The dice markings are 1 opposite 2, 3 opposite 4, and 5 opposite 6, unlike in later dices where the sum total of opposite numbers makes seven. The toys included animal figures with movable heads. The detachable arms of a human figure in stone have also been found at Lothal.

Man vs. Nature

Lothal is an epitome of man's struggle to meet the challenge of nature and build a prosperous society which he did effectively and enjoyed it for five centuries but gradually lost the strength to fight natural calamities. He had to retire from the scene, but not without making substantial contribution to human progress. Lothal is the earliest planned port town with a scientifically designed tidal dock of the world which gave a great filip to overseas trade and safer berthing for sea-going vessels. It added a maritime province to the Indus empire which was built on economic foundation rather than military force. The second contribution of Lothal to human progress is the invention of a simple alphabetic writing in which the languages of the Indo-Aryans and Indo-Iranians could be expressed. It also contributed to the development of Semitic and Brahmi alphabets.

MATHURA, THE LAND OF SRI KRISHNA'S BIRTH (Krishna Janmabhumi)

In 1959, I held charge of the excavations branch at Nagpur and was subsequently transferred to Agra circle in 1960. Before settling down at Agra, I received a telegram from the secretary for culture, UP government, Lucknow asking me to inspect and report whether some Muslim graves in ancient Katra Kesav Dev, site of Krishna's birth at Mathura, were disturbed as complained by local Muslims. Next day I went to Mathura and found the complaint was baseless. The secretary of the Krishna Janmabhumi Trust, Sri Sastry told me that some *goondas* placed a few bricks on the holy land of Krishna's birth which belonged to the Janmabhumi Trust. Their intention was to obstruct the construction of the temple on the holy land. As I found no evidence of any graves existing there, I recorded the complaint as baseless and proceeded to Deeg to inspect the palace which was protected by ASI. A few months later I was asked to demarcate the land proposed to be acquired from the Trust area for protecting the Idgah at Mathura. I reported that the Trust land cannot be acquired. The propasal was dropped after the then speaker of the Parliament, who was also the president of the Janmabhumi Trust, questioned the wisdom of acquiring the holy land of the Trust. Every year during my tenure in Agra and Delhi, I with my family members used to attend the Janmashtami festival at Mathura and Brindavan, as well as Gokul and Govardhana Hill. I also undertook repairs to the ancient temple of Madan Mohan (Krishna) on the Yamuna at Brindavan.

KAUSAMBI – GHOSHITARAMA

At the invitation of Prof. G.R. Sharma I went from Agra to Allahabad and proceeded with him to Kausambi where excavation was in progress. We reached the excavated site Kausambi, which had a history dating back to the period of the Mahabharata. The ancient text says that after Hastinapura was destroyed by floods, the ruler and the ruled left for Kausambi. This site later occupied by Buddhists was famous for the monastery of Ghoshitarama, which Sharma had laid bare. His excavation has yielded pre-Mauryan artefacts also.

The fine specimens of ceramic ware of the Mauryan period – known as the Northern Black Polished Ware – are found in Kausambi in well dated levels. This ware has a wide distribution all over northern India. Its occurrence at any site serves as a datum line for 5th century BC to 2nd century AD period in the absence of other datable finds.

DISCOVERY OF PRE-HISTORIC ROCK PAINTINGS

In one of my visits to the monuments in Rewa district of Madhya Pradesh, I made it a point to explore pre-historic sites. One such site discovered is Itar Pahar Hills. Here I came across ten pre-historic rock shelters with paintings (Fig. 19) in red. They are superimposed on the earlier paintings in white. In the shelter there were microliths too. Elated by the discovery, I spent more time late in the evening and left for Allahabad. On the way I started driving the jeep which had a heavily loaded trailer too. Suddenly on

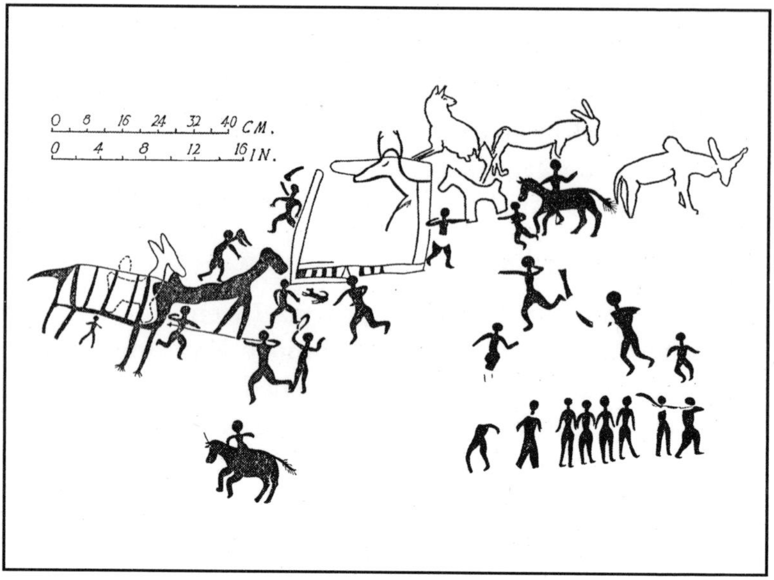

Fig. 19. Rock painting in Itar Pahar, Reva District.

seeing the railway level crossing without light and the gate closed and unable to stop the vehicle, I could only pray to Lord Krishna to save us. The jeep dashed against the wicket gate, the tyres burst and the vehicle came to a dead stop but thankfully we were saved.

VISIT TO THE HOLY SHRINE OF BADRINATH

I accompanied the Deputy Minister, Mr. Manmohan Das, to Hardwar and then to Joshi Math. But the minister, who fell sick, could not continue the journey further to Badrinath. I stayed back at Srinagar and asked my wife and children to join me. On their arrival next day, we drove through winding narrow roads, with the sub- Himalayan mountain soaring in the sky on one side and the Alaknanda (Ganga) River roaring in the valley 2000 feet below. The driver was an expert in negotiating the hilly track. We crossed the hanging bridge, *Lakshman Jhula.* After a descent to 2000 feet, we had to climb to 12000 feet, but there was no road except a 4 feet wide bridle path along the edge of the mountains. We took the ponies to reach our destination, the holy shrine of Badrinath. Each one of us had a separate pony to ride. On the way we visited the temples at Gopeswar and Pandukeswar, both under repairs by ASI. The problem with Pandukeswar temple was that its roof was leaking because the concrete had not set due to snowfall. This was a new experience to archaeological conservators unaccustomed to sub-Himalayan regions of snowfall. As we proceeded further, we had to halt at Hanumanchetty as the narrow bridge ahead on a rivulet had collapsed. Fortunately emergency repairs were carried out by the Border Road Organisation in view of the fact that the President of India, Babu Rajendra Prasad was returning from Badrinath.

We reached Badrinath in the evening. It was soothing to take a bath in the hot water spring amidst biting cold. Next morning we performed a *puja* in the temple of Vishnu (Badrinath). The priest was a Namboodiri from Kerala. After a hearty meal of rice, *dal* and *chapati* prepared by my Nepali cook, we went up to Manali, where we were shown the camping site of Chinese soldiers. Next day as we left the temple after morning *puja*, we met the chairman of Badrinath temple committee. He was impressed by a Sanskrit verse sung by a eight-year old Gopal. It conveyed the sense that "non-violence, control of the senses, compassion for all living beings, truth, knowledge, meditation and doing one's duty are the eight flowers of worship which please the God". The chairman was very happy and garlanded Gopal. On our return journey, we conducted among ourselves the *antyakshari* which involves singing songs by two groups. The last syllable of a song sung by the first group should serve as the first syllable of the song to be sung by the second group. This encourages children to learn new songs and *slokas* and also instills a spirit of competition. My next visit to Badrinath with my brother Ramachandra in a bad season was more adventurous. It was raining and the road from Joshimath onward was slushy and while crossing a flooded rivulet on a wooden plank, the horse slipped and fell in the gushing stream. With great difficulty we could save the horse by pulling it to shore.

5

Study Tour Abroad

In the course of my study of Lothal antiquities, I found evidence of the cultural contact of Lothal with Sumerian civilisation. The maritime contact of Lothal with Bahrain, Oman, Egypt, Ur, Kish, Ugarit and Susa necessitated a closer study of West Asian antiquities in the museums of UK, France, Germany and Cairo. Under the Cultural Exchange Programme, I was deputed to France for study in Sorbonne in 1961, under the guidance of Prof. Claude Schaeffeur, who was a member of the French Academy. Although Prof. Schaeffeur was busy writing the final report of his excavations at the Biblical site of Ugarit, he could spare time for me for discussions with him. I could study the antiquities in the Louvre Museum, especially those of Ghirsman's excavation in Iran and Syria, as well as those from Egypt. The British Museum collection of antiquities from Max Mallowan's excavation in Iraq was also valuable for my study. The West Asian antiquities here, from excavations at Susa and Sialk, showed some analogy with those of Lothal. I noticed that some of the pottery shapes of the late and post-Harappan and other Chalcolthic sites such as Navda Toli and Daimabad in India resembled the channel spouted vessels of Sialk. Among painted motifs, a man leading a horse, a lion drawn in dots on the pottery of Daimaad were also comparable to those from Sialk and Susa. I could also study Phoenican antiquities from Sidon, Tyre, Tripoli, Rouad and Toulose. A brief account of my study of pre-historic and proto-historic antiquites in Europe may interest the reader.

On my arrival at Paris, Madame Odette Viennot and Mr. Viennot met me and made arrangements for my stay at Hotel Raneleigh. As an art historian, Ms. Viennot had studied Indian art and therefore took interest in my studies. I also visited *Musee des Beaux Arts et Prehisoire* at Angouleume in April 1961. After Angouleume I visited Cave La Moustere, about 10 km from Les Elysie. This gave me an idea of the pre-historic rock paintings, tools and weapons. The curator explained the conservation measures taken to preserve the rock paintings.

The Museum of Perigord has fine specimens of Acheulian industry from Acheul on the River Sonne. At the Grand Roc, the crystalline formations and grottos attract many tourists, especially the amegdoloid formations, and *In Lagerie,* the rock paintings and sections of habitation deposits about 6 m thick are well preserved. I took the opportunity to study Cave Moustere, near Les Eysies, where rock paintings and pre-historic tools are in situ.

MUSEE DE L' HOMME, PARIS

The anthropological and ethnological sections of this premier museum of man are worth a great deal of study. Graduate students of pre-history from all over the world find it useful to study the evolution of man and division of races as then known to anthropologists.

OTHER SITES AND MUSEUMS IN FRANCE

My visit to Renne was useful for a study of pre-historic and Roman antiquities. Before I could go to the museum, I struggled hard to find a place for lodging. In three hotels, I was told 'toute complete' (all full). At the fourth hotel, the manager asked me if I was an Italian. I replied, "I am an Indian." He jumped with joy and said, "Oh Gandhi, Nehru" and gave me a room instantly. I was happy to know that India was held in high regard here. In Paris, Mr. Larouch, assistant curator of Louvre, was an admirer of Gandhi. He helped me to study the antiquities. Prof. Philip Stern, director of Musee Guimet, presided over my lecture in the Museum on Lothal excavation.

ROME

I was invited by Prof. Guiseppe Tucci, the renowned Indologist and director of ISMEO in Rome, to deliver a lecture on Lothal which had received considerable publicity as a result of two articles by me on Lothal excavations published in the *Illustrated London News* of February and March 1961 issues. Later on, in 1969, the French magazine *Archaeologiia* published in its May-June 1969 issue my article on Lothal, a port city of the Indus Valley civilisation. My lecture at ISMEO was well attended by professors from various universities in Italy.

A brief talk by me on Lothal was arranged and later when he received my report on excavations at Rangpur in *(Ancient_India No. 18-19, ASI),* he paid glowing tributes by saying that it is a model report.

LONDON

I made an in-depth study of the West Asian antiquities in the British Museum, London. So far as the Sumerian and Akkadian civilisations were concerned, Prof. Max

Mallowan spared time for discussions with me every Friday for an hour. In the Institute of Archaeology of the University of London, I had access to the large collection of antiquities from Brak, Ur, Kish, Arpachiya and Babylon. I found that the art and script of the Indus civilisation were distinct from those of Sumerian, Akkadian, Egyptian and Elamite civilisations. In town-planning too the Indus cities were different. Durrani from Pakistan and I went together to meet Wheeler in the British Academy. Later, he remarked, "Archaeologists can bring together India and Pakistan." In the course of my discussion on dating Indus civilisation, Wheeler never agreed with F.R. Allchin who had suggested a shorter chronology [see his foreword to my book, *Lothal and the Indus Civilisation* (1973)].

Wheeler, who agreed with my dating of Indus civilisation, wrote,

> The often-repeated nonsense about the Indus civilisation dating from, say 2100 to 1700 BC must be forgotten. As Sri Rao more than once implies, comparison where possible with established Mesopotamian historical dates is still the surer method. If we add the compact and rational shape of the town's layout, its regimented housing, its palace, its ventilated warehouse and, not least (and without doubt) its unique dock we may welcome in the present report a wholly unusual and complete presentation of Harappan life on its seaward fringe round about the end of the 3rd millennium.

Prof. F.E. Zeuner had introduced me in India to the study of geochronology, especially the role of interglacials and pluvials in determining the development of pre-historic cultures. In London he took some of the students of the Institute of Archaeology to Devils Dyke. Zeuner arranged my talk on Lothal excavations and a film show at the Institute of Archaeology, which was attended by Wheeler, Allchins and others. At a lunch given by Prof. Zeuner, we discussed the carbon 14 dates for Phase V, penultimate

Phase IV and mature phase III of Lothal and also the effect of floods in the nearby river which sealed the fate of Lothal in its closing days. Prof. Zeuner had examined the soil samples from the cutting in the river-bed.

EGYPTIAN MONUMENTS

One of the earliest at Giza I could see how a civilisation so great as the Egyptian got buried in the sands of the desert. Here were the Great Pyramids of the Fourth Dynasty datable to 2601-2525 BC. The three granite pyramids erected by Menkaure Khafre and Khufu, rise to a height of 450 ft. The tomb chambers are not easily accessible. For some centuries the tombs were mistaken for granaries as the chambers were empty. The narrow steep passage which led to the chamber in the heart of the mass of stone masonry of the pyramid was sealed so that none could trace or rob the chamber. Three other false passageways misled the robbers. But some treasure hunters did find the real passage and robbed the tomb of Khufus. Lying on my belly, I crawled through the dark passage and reached the tomb chamber. The Cairo Museum houses the treasures of Tutankhamen and other rulers. Precious stone and gold were lavishly used in decorating the tomb chamber. In Saqqara, the Fifth Dynasty tomb has beautiful painted limestone reliefs depicting, among others, a scene of hunting rhinoceros. When I was working in Sorbonne at College de France, the Epigraphist Naugayrol had explained to me how the inscriptions on the famous Rosetta Stone (the original lying in the British Museum, London) were deciphered by Jean Francois Champollion (1790-1832) who could locate the names, Ptolemy and Cleopatra, in the Egyptian scripts. There are three inscriptions on the Rosetta stone, namely, (1) The hieroglyphic (from the Greek word *hieros*, 'sacred' and *glyphein*, 'to carve'), (2) The pictographic – some of the symbols are pictures similar to the Sumerian symbols, and

(3) The demotic (of 8th century BC) named as such from *demos*, 'the people'. In course of time the hieroglyphic script developed into hieratic, a simplified form of hieroglyphic, enabling the scribes to write quickly on papyrus. From 8th century BC onward, all the three systems of writing were in use, each for a specific use. Religious texts were written in hieratic inscriptions and on monuments in heiroglyphic, and the rest in demotic. The Egyptian language died out as Greek became popular in the 4th century BC.

Apart from the excavated tombs in the Valley of Kings further south of Giza, the most impressive edifice is the Great Temple of Amun at Karnak. One wonders how the massive round columns and the stone blocks could be put in position without mechanical aid. The pylon of Remeses II with the famous obelisk in front of the temple of Amun Mut and Khonsu (Luxor, 1279-1212) are noteworthy. The funerary temple of Queen Hatshepsut (1478-1458 BC) at Deir-al-Bahri is no less significant here. A set of gamesmen closely analogous to the one from Lothal has been found here. She was not just a queen but also a living god. I saw her statue which is in the Metropolitan Museum of New York during my subsequent visit to USA. I had a pleasant surprise at Cairo where Mr. Rao of Indian embassy invited me for dinner. I felt happy when Indian food was offered to me by Mrs. Rao on one condition that I must speak to Rao and his wife in Kannada only. This was a welcome bonus.

KAVERIPATNAM – TAMIL NADU

My colleague in the survey, Mr. K.V. Raman found in the Manigramam suburb and in the Pallavanesvaram temple grove antiquities of early Chola times, which led us to identify ancient sites here. Further excavation in the buried ancient channel of River Kaveri revealed a brick wharf of 3rd century BC and a Buddha *vihara* in Kaveripatnam habitation area establishing thereby that Kaveripatnam was a flourishing port much earlier than the Sangam Period (1st century AD).

DISCOVERY OF PAIYAMPALLI

The Neolithic site at Paiyampalli, also known as Baiyanapalli, in Jalarpet Taluk of North Arcot district of Tamil Nadu was discovered when we stopped for a while at the suggestion of my daughter, Nalini to explore the foot of the hill where pottery and neoliths were found. This site is situated on the Madras-Krishnagiri highway. During a preliminary survey, I collected a few sherds of Grey and Black and Red Ware pottery and also a broken polished stone axe. After seeing them Nalini seriously asked me how I could guess this to be a Neolithic site. I pointed out to her the dwelling places of Neolithic folk, namely, the rock shelters occupied by people who could undertake insipid cultivation in the terrace below. The Grey Ware and Neolithic stone tool found here indicated the site was 3000 years old. The Black and Red pottery of Megalithic culure was also found at the site. After realising the necessity of obtaining firm dates for Neolithic cultures, the excavation of Paiyampalli was started in 1964 and continued through 1965, even after I assumed charge of the post of deputy director-general of ASI at Delhi. The site has yielded evidence of two phases of Neolithic culture, the first one of cave-dwellings and the second pit-dwelling in open terrace. The Neolithic culture could be dated to 1600-1200 BC by 14C dating method, while the Megalithic burials and habitation were assigned to 600-200 BC. A footed sarcophagus of terracotta found in the Megalithic burial at the site contained human bones, iron arrowheads and Black-and-Red ware (*Indian Archaeology: A Review 1963-64, 64-65*).

The iron industry in Komaranahalli in Karnataka has been dated by A. Sundara to 1300 BC, while Gufkral in

Kashmir has yielded iron objects in Megalithic levels datable to 15th century BC. The dating of iron and the introduction of iron technology in India is of primary importance to the proto-history of India, especially for dating *Mahabharata* according to which iron weapons were used in the battle of Kurukshetra. Recently, the excavation at Malhar in Chandauli district of UP has yielded iron tools in levels dated 1600 BC.

ARCHAEOLOIGICAL SITES IN USSR

Under the Cultural Exchange Programme of India and USSR, I and my colleague, Z.A. Desai, an expert in Muslim epigraphy, were selected for study in the Soviet Union. When we reached Moscow on December 2, 1971, we were received by the staff of the Indian Embassy in Moscow and lodged in a Hotel. Next day we shifted to the Academy of Sciences Guest House where Zednoprovosky, a laison officer from the department of culture met us. Thereafter we had no problems. Despite heavy snowfall, I ventured to go out and see the city and experienced the terrible Russian cold. While standing in the que for an hour in the snow, my feet were getting numb. I kept moving my legs lest I should suffer from frostbite. Somehow I could visit the Kremlin, the Cathedral of Annunciation and the Cathedral in the Red Square, as well as the church of Holy Trinity built in 1643. From Moscow we went to Leningrad by train and Zednoprovisky took me to the Academy of Sciences. The Hermitage was the most impressive museum that I saw in Russia. What struck me most was the *Gitopadesa* scene carved in sandalwood from Mysore exhibited in the Indian Gallery where children were explained the significance of the exhibit and India's contribution to world art and culture. Of course, neither religion nor philosophy was highlighted.

From the Academy of Sciences in Leningrad, one could see icebergs moving slowly in the river. The temperature outside was 10 degrees F below normal. In the Academy Prof. Knorozov who was working on Indus script, which he had computerised, was very helpful in explaining to me the structural analysis of the script he had underaken. N. Gurov, who had visited India a number of times and also knew South Indian languages well, had come forward with the theory that Indus language was proto-Dravidian. During my lecture arranged in the Leningrad (Now St. Petersberg) University, Zednoprovosky, Gurov and Knorozov were present. I explained that the Indus script was neither a pictograph nor an ideograph but had evolved into a phonetic script in late levels. My analysis and comparison of Indus cursive signs with Semitic signs confirmed it. The reading of the inscriptions revealed that Indus language was close to Old Indo-Aryan. Prof. Ivanov, an expert on Indo-European languages, appreciated my analysis of the script.

I was surprised to find one midnight Prof. Knorozov tapping the door of my room in the Academy. He did not know English to the extent of expressing clearly his ideas. However, he had brought a message to me, perhaps at the instance of some higher authority. He said, "Russia will stand shoulder to shoulder with India in its effort to give East Pakistan freedom." The war had broken out the same day. Within a few days when the Pakistani general surrendered to the Indian general, the vice president of the Academy of Sciences at Tashkent told me that we should celebrate the occasion. It is well known how the Soviet Union helped India win the war.

I visited a few monuments in Ashkabad, Samarkand and Bokhara. In one of the museums, a painting which depicted the horrors committed by Chengeze Khan was prominently displayed. The conservation of ancient monuments such as the Sarai and a minar in Bokhara was impressive. A leaning tower has been restored to plumb by slowly moving inch-by-inch the steel frame in which the tower was tightly set. In Bokhara, some of the factories which had caused pollution were removed to save the ancient monuments. These and other measures taken by USSR government confirm their interest in preserving the heritage of man.

The Bronze Age Museum at Bilisi, in the Georgian Republic is noted for its excellent collection of stone and metal objects. Here I had to stand for 6 to 7 hours daily taking down notes on the antiquities which were not allowed to be taken out of the showcases. During my visits, one of the professors asked me how I could get enough energy to work so hard without taking any non-vegetarian food and spirituous liquor. I told him that practising yoga helps one to get more energy. I narrated the benefits of *pranayama* and meditation. Since they did not believe in God, they thought they could not practise yoga. But yoga is a technique of self-control leading to concentration of mind which needs no God. I do not know whether they were impressed by my explanation.

Certain aspects of the Soviet Union impressed me. Food was simple and cheap; there was hardly any unemployment. Of course every able-bodied person had to work. Education and other needs of the children were taken care of by the state. Our guide, Mr. Ahmad in Takshkent told me that he and his wife earned enough and the child was looked after by the state, and his surplus money was spent on drinks. One of the achievements of the Soviet Union was the drastic reduction in the disparity between the rich and the poor. The principle "either all will have it or none" was followed in letter and spirit. For instance, in a departmental store in Leningrad, I was told that soluble coffee was introduced for some time, but they could not meet the demand in full and hence withdrew soluble coffee.

Most consumer products were cheap, because the factories could avoid expenditure on advertisement of goods. The transport system in cities by bus and train was convenient. The people were courteous and very helpful.

While at Aurangabad, I had a long discussion with Prof. D. Schlingloff and his wife regarding the identification of some of the panels in Ajanta paintings. Prof. Schlingloff has published his new interpretation of the *Jataka* stories of Ajanta under the title, *die identifizierrng einer Ajantamalerie* (1977).

The Bangalore circle of ASI was formed in 1976 after a great deal of effort. The Governor, Mr. Dharmavira did his best to expedite formation of the circle. The first thing I did was to hold an exhibition of sculptures and photographs of monuments to create awareness of our cultural heritage in Karnataka.

During my tenure at Bangalore, the director of the Max Muller Bhavan was kind enough to get an invitation for me to visit departments of Indian Studies in the universities of Munich, Hamburg, Bonn and Kiel. Initially there was some difficulty in my obtaining permission from the government of India to go to Germany (FRG) because of emergency. Luckily, Mr. H.Y. Sharada Prasad, information adviser to Prime Minister Indira Gandhi, could obtain clearance for my visit. A lecture by me on Indus script and language was arranged by Prof. Schlingloff in Munich and by Dr. Hartel in the Berlin Museum of Indian Art. As a result of my discussion with Prof. Paul Thieme in Tubingen I got some doubts cleared regarding the affinity of the Indus language with old Indo-Aryan. Prof. Steitencron too participated in the discussion. Prof. Wezler in Hiedelberg and other scholars were interested in my decipherment of the Indus script and the identification of the language as old Indo-Aryan.

In November 1977, I was awarded the prestigeous Jawaharlal Nehru Fellowship, for undertaking further research on Indus civilisation and Indus script. This gave me enough time and library facilities to continue my research on the Indus script.

The Ford Foundation of USA offered a travel grant for visiting a few universities where research on ancient languages was in progress. I preferred the Oriental Institute, Chicago, the Pennsylvania and Boston Universities for research. I had a long discussion with Prof. I.J. Gelf on my decipherment.

In the light of the new evidence of evolution of Indus script, he held that my methodology was more appropriate.

Education of Children

My son Gopal studied for his Indian School Certificate examination in Delhi and then appeared at the All India entrance examination for admission to the Indian Institute of Technology, Madras. After a few months of study in IIT, he was admitted in the hospital for typhoid. At Aurangabad, Kamala and I were anxious about Gopal's health and prayed continuously for his recovery. Shakuntala who was attending on him assured us that Gopal's temperature was normal but he was weak. I went to Madras IIT hostel to take care of him. He recovered fast and attended his examination too. Nalini had joined B.A. course in Marathawada University at Aurangabad. She was a good debater and participated in inter-collegiate debates with enthusiasm and conviction. For the college day she participated in the Sanskrit drama *Mricchakatika* (Clay Cart). But a more memorable occasion was when she performed a Bharatnatyam dance on stage, Gopal played on the tabla, Shakuntala and Kamala sang the song and gave the beat. During holidays, I took my family members to historical places, such as Ajanta, Ellora, Elephanta, Shanwarwada, Fathehpur Sikri, Lucknow, Mathura, Benaras, and Dwarka which created interest among them in Indian art and culture.

6

Conservation of Major Monuments

CONSERVATION OF MONUMENTS IN RAJASTHAN

CHITTORGARH: A SYMBOL OF RESISTANCE TO FOREIGN INVASION

The fort of Chittor situated in Udaipur divsion of Rajasthan is famous for monuments which speak of the heroic deeds of Rana Pratap, the famous Rajput ruler of Mewad who fought relentlessly with the army of Akbar and refused to accept the suzerainty of the Mughal emperor. After he lost the battle of Haldighati, Rana Pratap made Kumbhalgarh hill fort his capital.

It was not merely the Rajput rulers but also their subjects who fought for preseving the independence of their kingdoms. After Rana Pratap left Chittorgarh, the blacksmiths who manufactured and supplied to Rana Pratap the spears, swords and shields necessary for war also abandoned Chittor and swore that they would not return to Mewad until it regained independence. These itinerant smiths (*gadi lohads*) moving in bullock carts from one village to another earned their living by repairing agricultural implements.

NEHRU VISITS CHITTOR (Fig. 20)

After India gained independence, the *gadi lohads* agreed to return to Chittor. It was arranged that seven chief ministers and the prime minister of India were to receive the *gadi lohads* at seven gates of Chittor fort and the prime minister would address them. The joint director-general of archaeology at Delhi, T.N. Ramachandran wanted that the Prime Minister Jawaharlal Nehru, the author of the *Discovery of India,* should see the seals and other antiquities of Indus Valley civilisation recently discovered at Lothal. He requested the prime minister to open the exhibition of Lothal Antiquities to be set up by me at Chittorgarh on the occasion of the prime minister's visit for the celebration of *gadi lohad's* formal re-entry into Chittorgarh. The prime minister who had seen earlier Mohenjodaro readily agreed to open the exhibition. We displayed Indus seals, jewellery, stone weights, copper tools and models of the excavated

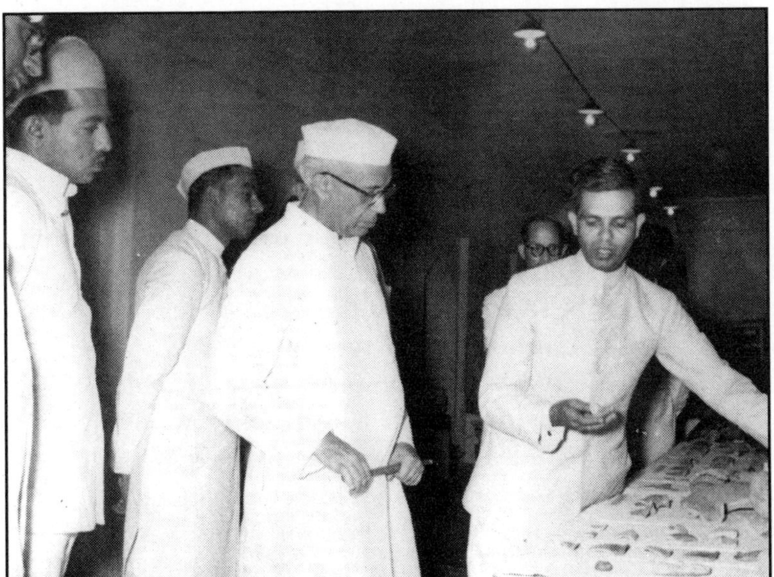

Fig. 20. Nehru visits Lothal exhibition in Chittorgarh.

buildings and the cemetery of Lothal. Along with the prime minister came other chief ministers, namely, Morarji Desai from Bombay (now Mumbai), Ravishankar Shukla from Nagpur, Sukhadia from Jaipur, the Rana of Mewad and other dignitaries who were greatly interested in the exhibition. Nehru was happy that post-partition India could find a prosperous Indus Valley port town within its borders. He put some searching questions to me about the unique writing of the Harappans. I explained its significance. Before opening the exhibition I had accompanied the prime minister to important monuments, including Padmini's Palace and Mira's temple repaired by ASI. At the temple Nehru listened to Mira's devotional songs sung by a blind devotee.

When the ASI took over the monuments of Chittorgarh, they were in ruins but we had to repair the more important ones, namely, the palaces of Fatta, Rana Kumbha, Padmini, Rana Ratan Singh, as well as the Tower of Victory built by Rana Kumbha, the Tower of Fame, and temples of Sammidheswar, Kalikamata and the *sati* enclosure, where Rajput ladies resorted to self-immolation to avoid molestation.

Mahanaleswara Temples

This group of temples in Udaipur district of Rajasthan includes subsidary shrines and a well decorated with sculptures. In the same complex there is a *Matha (monastery)* and a rock inscription. The River Menal takes a leap of 100 m from the rocky edge on either side of which a few medieval temples are built. The thickly wooded hill, waterfalls, and temples make Menal a unique religious centre of tourist interest as well as architectural beauty. It was unapproachable in 1956 for lack of proper road from Chittor via Bijolia where again there are several beautiful temples and inscriptions. In order to protect and repair these temples, I went to Menal from Bijolia accompanied by Sengupta, a senior conservator, Suyal, Junior Conservator, N.C. Shah, photographer and Vadnerkar, stenographer. It had rained heavily the previous night, which helped us to locate leaking spots in the ceiling of the temple. While examining the leaky roof, a saffron-clad saint came in and made enquiries about the temple. Later I came to know that he was none other than the famous Saint Tukadoji Maharaj of Nagpur who on that day was observing silence *(mauna)*. An hour later he broke his silence and asked me who I was and what I intended to do about these long neglected temples. I told him that the ASI intends to repair the temples which are yet to be protected under AMASR Act. He asked me, "How much time do you take to repair them?" I replied, "One year for some urgent measures of conservation." He remarked, "one year in government terminology means several years." I was not disturbed by this retort. Sengupta and Suyal looked at me. I accepted the challenge. Later the saint asked his disciple to give us some sweets *(laddus)*. We thanked him and ate the *laddus* sitting on the rock overlooking the waterfall. Our hunger being satisfied, we discussed repairs. As the Menal temples were not protected, we could not spend much money without the director-general's sanction. Moreover, funds were limited. There was not even a watchman in this tiger-infested forest area to look after the monuments and their exceedingly beautiful sculptures, but I had an excellent team of wokers motivated to take up any work anywhere. I sent four masons and a watchman from Chittor with Mr. Suyal and made a small amount available to start structural repairs. This included water tightening the leaky roof after grouting cracks and resetting dislodged architectural members. Among sculptures there was one of a bird picking up water drops from the wet hair of a lady taking her bath, as described in ancient Sanskrit works.

It was getting dark when we left Menal for Bijolia after the villagers on the way asked us to take a shorter route to Bijolia up the hill instead of going round the hill and assured us that "Rajasaheb's vehicle (*gadi*) also goes that way." We took the hilly route and soon found to our dismay that the road was full of pits and rubble. Sen Gupta and I alighted from the jeep and kept stones under the hind wheels to prevent sliding back. Tej Singh, the attendant, was in the front giving directions to driver Babu Rao. In darkness he was throwing some stones sideways, saying that he saw a tiger. Indeed, a tiger was following us in the bushes down the slope. Quickly we both jumped into the jeep and asked Tej Singh to do the same.

On an earlier occasion, when I was driving an open jeep at midnight from Kota Railway Station to Badoli in Kota division of Rajasthan, we had to face a tiger and two cubs near Badoli. I got scared to drive further, lest the jeep should run over the cubs. The driver Babu Rao quickly took the steering and drove fast without any fear. We reached our destination safely. Next morning, while narrating our experience to the watchman of the temple he related his own experience of a tiger hiding in a bush near the temple. Fortunately it ran away after he set fire to a bush. Later, we provided him with a gun.

THE TAJ MAHAL (Fig. 21A-B)

The Taj Mahal, a tomb built by Emperor Shah Jahan, at Agra was in need of repairs. Its double dome presented some problems. Salt had been affecting the intradose of the dome and the plaster was peeling off. A large number of cracks were also appearing in the ceiling of the vault of the underground chamber. Moreover, the iron dowels used for fixing the marble veneering of the dome had rusted. The expert committee consisting of the director-general of ASI, the chief engineer of Central Public Works Department and

Fig. 21a. The Taj Mahal in moonlight.

the archaeological chemist, had recommended certain remedial measures and the recommendations had to be implemented by me assisted by Sen Gupta. The problem of likely erosion of the base of the stone platform on which the superstructure of Taj stands was solved by providing boulder pitching on the river bank. The excavations in the river bed were undertaken to ascertain if there was any disturbance of the foundation. The excavations revealed well-like constructions of rubble masonry at three places along the river bank below the platform (Fig. 21b). They were encased in wooden planks which were still intact. Boulder pitching recommended by the expert committee ensured the gradual diversion of the river current away from the platforms, and deposition of silt along its base took place. A few days later, a mild tremor occurred at night

Fig. 21b. Structural supports in river bed to the foundation of the platform of the Taj Mahal.

but the hairbreadth cracks in the walls and ceiling of the underground chamber were not disturbed nor were the glass tell-tales fixed on them dislodged. All that was needed was grouting as suggested by the Committee since the cracks were superficial . The marble slabs in the veneer of the dome damaged by rusted iron clamps were replaced by fresh marble slabs obtained from Makrana quarry matching with the original ones. The salt deposited by capillary action in the intradose of the dome was removed by the ASI chemist by paper pulp treatment and fresh plaster was applied. And these measures gave a longer lease of life to the Taj Mahal. Repairs to the famous tomb of the Sufi Saint Shaikh Salim Chishti at Fatehpur Sikri were also undertaken.

I took charge of the major excavation branch of ASI at Nagpur in January 1967 and surveyed the Buddhist site of Pauni in Maharashtra, and a few Neolithic sites in Andhra and Karnataka. The Neolithic site of Paiyampalli (Tamil Nadu) and Sivavaram in Andhra where Harappan wheel-like steatite beads were found was subsequently excavated. In the course of exploration of Kolar district in January 1968, a megalithic site, namely, Kendatti and Banahalli, a neolithic chalcolithic site, were discovered. It was also possible to determine the date of Neolithic culture as 1600 BC and Megalithic as 800 BC.

CONSERVATION OF MONUMENTS IN KARNATAKA AND MAHARASHTRA

ELLORA CAVES

There are in all 33 rock-cut temples scooped out of a massive hill of Deccan trap. They belong to Hindu, Buddhist and Jain faiths. The most famous among them is the temple of Kailasanatha (Cave No. 16). Both in conception and design, this massive rock-cut temple symbolising mythical Kailas, the abode of Lord Siva, excavated by the Rashtrakuta king Krishna I (AD 765-774), is one of the wonders of the world. It closely follows in plan and elevation the Early Chalukyan structural temple of Virupaksha (AD 740) at Pattadakal. The Kailasa temple consists of a gateway (*Gopura*), a cloistered large courtyard at ground level, a *Nandimantapa* and Siva shrine at higher level. In the courtyard measuring 276 ft. deep and 154 ft. wide are two free-standing monolithic shafts flanking the *Nandimantapa* and two massive figures of elephant. Around the open courtyard are a large number of niches, cut into the backdrop of 120 ft. mass of rock. Each panel depicting various activities of Siva and the major incarnations of Vishnu carved in bold relief is a masterpiece of art. The sculptures of Ellora are full of expression and force following the Early Chalukya scruptural art of Badami Caves. Among them, the *Ravananugraha murti* and the scene of Ravana shaking Kailasa are most noteworthy. In the latter, Ravana seated in *Virasana* is shaking the mount

Kailasa in which Siva is seated unpurturbed, and Parvati, slightly worried, is hugging him. The *Ganas* and Parvati's lady in-waiting are fleeing. Here the artist is creating an illusion of space. The reflected sunlight at different times creates an illusion of movement of the figures. The main shrine and the assembly hall are in the upper storey which is reached by a flight of steps. This needs an explanation because the architect must have conceived of different levels of spiritual experience on the part of the devotee. At the ground level the devotee is still in the mundane world enjoying the pleasures of wealth, power and love. Wealth is symbolised by *Sankhanidhi* and *Padmanidhi* flanking the gateway. To the right of a beautiful panel of the goddess of wealth Gajalakshmi behind the gate are Kama and Rati – embodiments of love. Next the devotee has to take a turn to see the river goddesses Ganga, Yamuna and Sarasvati symbolising purity of body and mind.

Further, as the visitor goes up a few steps he sees the *Sivalila* scenes and incarnations of Vishnu and finally *Kāla* (time) destroying the illusory world. The devotee is now spiritually elevated to reach the main shrine where he can meditate and concentrate on the uniconic (formless) God in the dark silent *garbhagriha* for attaining freedom from bondage (*moksha*).

I had the unique opportunity to carry out repairs to Ellora caves and also to re-install the fallen *linga* in the Kailas temple. Excavation carried out in front of Cave 16, where the founder of the *Mahanubhava* sect is said to have undertaken penance, did not yield much evidence except a platform. The followers of this sect are great devotees of Lord Krishna.

Symbolism in Indian Art

Indian art is intellectually demanding, but the early western critics of Indian art could neither understand the sprituality of Indian art nor its symbolism. For instance, V.A. Smith wrote, "Indian art could not express human passions" although by that time Ajanta paintings had been discovered. John Ruskin considered Indian art as monstrous and grotesque (Ray, N.R., 1974). It was left to A.K. Coomaraswamy and others like Stella Kramrisch to lay emphasis on the spiritual content of Indian art and the realism of the sculptural art in Buddhist caves of Karle and Bhaja. Indian art in Ajanta and Ellora is symbolic standing for eternal philosophic truths of Hindusim, Buddhism and Jainism. For instance, while the *stupas* at Sarnath and elsewhere contain relics of the Buddha, the solid rock-cut *stupas* of Ajanta and Ellora carved in *chaitya* do not contain any relic. They are more a symbol of the *nirvana* of Buddha. Similarly, the railing motifs carved on the *stupa* at these sites demarcates symbolically the inner sacred space from the outer secular space even as the gateway of the temples does (Nalini Rao, 1997). The concept of boundaries continues in the *prākāras* of temples. The *rangoli* drawn by Hindu ladies also marks the sacred space.

In early Buddhism (Hinayana), the Buddha was not worshipped and hence not depicted in figural form. He was worshipped in symbolic form of *nandipada* (his footprints), Bodhi tree where he attained enlightenment and the empty throne. That the art form gradually followed function can be exemplified by the introduction of a circumambulatory passage *(pradakshinapatha)* in the *chaitya* to enable devotees to go round the *stupa*. Later on, in the Mahayana form of Buddhism, the figure of Buddha was incorporated with the *stupa* at Ajanta as well as Ellora. The figure of Buddha can be identified from the iconographic features, namely, *ushnisha* (signifying his second brain), the *urna* (dot or curl on his forehead), and *mudra* (hand gestures) indicating fearlessness (*abhaya*) or teaching (*vyakhyana)* or touching the earth (*bhumi sparsa)* as a witness to his attaining enlightenment.

Ajanta Caves

Problems of Conservation

The Ajanta caves discovered in 1819 were brought to the notice of archaeologists in 1843 by Fergusson. At the instance of the East India Company, R. Gill copied the paintings, but these copies were destroyed by a fire in 1866 in the Crystal Palace at Sydenham. Later, the students of J.J. School of Arts, Bombay prepared coloured copies under the direction of John Griffiths. The Ajanta paintings carry several narratives from the Buddhist *Jatakas* (stories of earlier births before becoming Buddha) wherein compassion, charity and other noble deeds are highlighted for the guidance of mankind. Ajanta is like a theatre inside the caves with beautifully dressed women in palaces and gardens besides scenes of men and women worshipping Buddha. Cave No. 10, the earliest (2nd century BC) is a *chaitya* hall of Hinayana Buddhism. Except for a royal scene the painting in it is damaged extensively. In caves 1, 2, 16 and 17 (of later date – 5th century AD), the paintings are fairly well preserved.

Initially, the erstwhile Hyderabad state took measures to clear the caves and also appointed Italian restorers to remove the coat of dust, dirt and varnish applied indiscriminately over the paintings. E.L. Vassey produced good colour photographs and Yazdani's portfolio of *Ajanta Paintings* is the most authentic. After the caves were taken over by ASI from Hyderabad state in 1951, the masonry pillars erected for supporting the overhanging rocks were replaced by mass concrete duly reinforced. But the major leakage of water over the paintings in the ceilings and walls of caves 1, 2, 16 and 17 had not stopped. The earlier measures such as providing drains in the hill slopes above the caves to ward off stagnation and seepage of water in the monsoon were not effective. In 1970 I surveyed the hill slopes thoroughly and located a couple of fissures in the rock through which water used to seep into caves. The exact spots in the ceiling of caves 1, 2, 16 and 17 where water appeared through the fissures above were marked for treatment by injecting grout in the fissures.

We grouted liquid cement in the fissures and repeated the process at intervals. As a result of this measure, it was found that leakage in caves 1, 2, 9, 10, 16, 17 stopped. In one single hole in the rock above the caves, 40 bags of cement were used for grouting. In the earlier attempt to trace points of seepage, water had appeared at 36 points in these and adjoining caves. The Ajanta Expert Committee which met in 1974 observed that there was no leakage after grouting in four caves.

Another problem was that the caves were infested with bats. This was stopped after certain measures were undertaken.The third problem related to chemical preservation of the paintings which was the responsibility of B.B. Lal, director, Science (Chief Archaeological Chemist), under whose direction Mathur and other chemists carried out cleaning and preservation of paintings. Removal of chalk appearing on the panel of *Sutasoma Jataka* in Cave 17 was done by the use of an organic solvent. The chemist felt that white incrustation may be due to the application of a polymer product as a preservative coat. The committee decided in 1974 that the treated portions of the painted surface should be left without any application and kept under watch for any recurrence of chalkiness of any preservative. After the whitish material is identified by BARC, a permanent cure was to be suggested. Leaving some parts untreated, rest of the painting was to be cleaned, and daily records of quantum of solvents and chemicals used were to be kept.

Fumigation was carried out in September 1974 in Cave 1 as an experiment. The painting in the left cell in Cave 11 containing *Yaksha* images was treated with 10% formalin in alcohol for exterminating insects in the holes. Later on, the holes and crevices were filled with plaster of Paris containing perytherum. The earlier experiment with sodium pentachlora phenol was not successful. In Cave 11, to eliminate proliferation of insect activity, such as boring holes by betels in the plaster of painting, the National Chemical Laboratory had suggested non-destructive and sensitive methods such as X-ray Fluorescene Spectroscopy and Neutron activation by labs of the Bhabha Atomic Research Centre. For the appearance of crackle or alegatering on painted surface, further study was recommended. Further, samples from 6 cm of rock in Cave 1 were examined earlier for determining moisture, temperature and permeability during and after monsoon. As a result of the examination of samples it was found that inside the cave the maximum temperature was 80 to 90 degrees F and minimum 67 to 86 F. In the caves visited by thousands of people daily, carbon dioxide and oxygen contents were noted. The Prime Minister Indira Gandhi had observed that if necessary we should not hesitate to close the caves to the public pending necessary arrangements. The Expert Committee, which studied the problems of Ajanta vis a vis those of Lascaux Caves in France, observed that "the appearence of green algae was the result of high occupancy in Lascaux Cave where the paintings are directly on the calcite rock and not on mud plaster, as in Ajanta, where the inner face of the rock carrier is rendered rough for providing a proper bond between the carrier and the plaster". This bond is still firm except in small areas where it is loose. The detachment is due to internal environmental condition of the cave. The ground of Ajanta paintings is composed of mud plaster containing about 10 to 12 per cent of combined water and organic matter such as vegetable fibre, paddy husk, grass, etc. besides rock grit or sand. The composition of the ground is 60 per cent silica and 27 per cent iron and alumina. Lime and magnesia account for 2 per cent. The ground was made of ferruginous earth, rock grit and vegetable material with hardly any lime, but traces of white layer below the pigment indicate presence of lime, kaolin or gypsum. The ground is soft and porous and does not possess the strength and durability of common lime plaster. The ground consisted of three layers, pigments, plaster, and course plaster.

A variety of pigments was used in painting, importantly yellow, red, blue, white, black and green, all of mineral origin. The technique of painting was not of *fresco buono,* but *tempera.*

Patan Devi Temple

This medieval temple situated 10 miles from Ellora had to be repaired after removing modern accretions but a young saint by name Pranavananda Sarasvati from Bengal who is a devotee of Goddess Kali lived here because this was the seat of the famous Mathematician-cum-Astronomer, Bhaskaracharya. The saint vacated the temple when I offered to repair it. An inscription of the grandson of Bhaskaracharya states that he established a college for the study of astronomy here. Our exploration of the nearby site yielded a sacrificial pit (*homa kunda*) of early medieval period at the site believed to be the seat of the great astronomer. After the necessary repairs were carried out, the Swamiji told me that I had restored the temple to the form he had seen in his dream on the first day after his initiation by the saint at Vajreswari near Bombay. In 1985 I met Pranavananda Saraswati again in a temple of Kali built by him in the village Patan. Unfortunately, he breathed his last a few years ago.

Mandapeswar

The Brahmanical rock-cut temple at Mandapeswar in Borivili near Mumbai was protected long ago by ASI, but it was being misused by the Jesuit Mission which had usurped 80 acres of land belonging to the temple. This monument was neglected by the ASI for long. The mission had erected several buildings and caused damage to the sculptures of Siva and other deities in the cave. In the course of conservation undertaken by me, I found that a damaged stone wall built to close the original sanctum had to be pulled down. As a result of this measure, an inscription mentioning the grant of land given to the temple of Mandapeswara was exposed on the door jamb of the cave. In the sanctum, the original *linga* was also found. The *Times of India*, Bombay published these discoveries. After prolonged litigation the mission on the advice of our solicitor Karl Khandalwala. conceded that it had no right on Mandapeswar temple, whereupon I could conserve some of the original features of the unique rock-cut temple in the suburb of Bombay city.

Kanheri Caves

In the course of conserving the damaged floor and walls of the Buddhist caves in Kanheri, near Mumbai, an interesting evidence of metal-smelting in furnaces came to light. A number of terracotta sealings of Nalanda seals used as prayer tablets bearing the figure of seated Buddha were also found. In the nearby cemetery, several Brahmi inscriptions and scenes from *Jataka* stories, carved on structural cemeteries, were recovered.

Raigadh Hill Fort of Shivaji

Among the major forces that could face Mughal incursion, Rana Pratap and Shivaji stand foremost. I undertook excavation in the citadel of Raigadh where the ministers of

Shivaji had their residence. The site where Shivaji's coronation took place was also conserved. I must mention here that my colleague 'Vidhwans' exerted himself in conserving Mandapeswar and Raigadh monuments, the latter situated on a hill top approachable only through a bridle path.

Badami, Cradle of Temple Architecture

The Malaprabha valley is truly the cradle of temple architecture in India. The Guptas in the north had no doubt constructed quite a few temples in the 5th century AD, but very few of them except those at Sanchi and Deogarh survived. Almost simultaneously the powerful Chalukyan rulers of the Malaprabha valley who built an empire in the South paid great attention to the construction of temples. It is in Aihole, Badami, Mahakuta and Pattadakal that under their patronage the local craftsmen and artists carried out great experiments in the construction of temples. The excavations at Aihole in 1969 yielded enough stratigraphic evidence to prove that the Gaudargudi, the earliest *mantapa* type of temple, was built in 5th century. The next stage of development of temple form can be seen in the Surya (Ladkhan) temple, wherein the pillared hall is enclosed by perforated screens. Here an attempt has been made by the builders to give a majestic look by adding an upper storey in the form of an upper shrine, but it is not yet incorporated in the main body fabric (*Lalit Kala* 15, 16). Further development to expand the structure vertically and horizontally can be traced in the lower and upper *Sivalayas* on the Badami hill. The culmination of the Southern Dravida Vimana and the Northern Rekhanagara styles is conspicuous in the Virupaksha and Kasi Visvesvara temples respectively at Pattadakal. The apsidal Durga temple of Aihole, which precedes the Virupaksha, is unique in plan and elevation with double ambulatory passages and profusely decorated pillars and niches (*devakoshtas*) in the walls. The curvilinear *sikhara* is a later addition.

In the Jaina temple on the hill at Aihole, attempts were made to enlarge the structure horizontally as well as vertically. Almost about this time, 7th century, the followers of Lakulisa cult built at Mahakuta small shrines on the bank of a small spring in Dravida Vimana and Rekhanagara styles.

The Chalukyan rulers who were followers of the Vaishnava cult patronised all faiths. They excavated exquisitely carved temples in the red sandstone hill at Badami (Vatapi), their capital. The earliest Vaishnava cave excavated by Pulakesi is dated to the 6th century. Scenes of *Krishṇalīlā* scenes from *Bhāgavata* are carved in relief in Cave3 and Mālegitti and upper *Sivalayas*. The incarnations of Vishnu as Varāha, Trivikrama, Ananta and Narasimha are among the finest relief sculptures noted for a new vigourous style. The dancing Siva (Naṭarāja) is another fascinating sculpture in Cave 1. Here sculptural art, monumental in size, becomes part and parcel of the architecture. At the same time the figures which are full of expression and force and noted for their composition and movement, reveal the greatness of the artists.

My first visit to Aihole, Pattadakal and Badami in 1967 gave me a shock because of the deplorable condition of more than 60 temples protected by ASI and completely neglected for 50 years. The approach to some temples was difficult. The first need was to get the original approaches cleared of hutments. The encroachment by local people had resulted in ugly constructions blocking the entrances. Manure pits were dug in front of the monuments. Some of the temples were occupied by villagers and used as cattle-sheds. Clearance of vegetation growth on temples took a year and structural repairs took another six years. Three special offices

Fig. 22. Excavation in Lad Khan (Surya) temple complex reveals a pre-6th century temple plinth, Aihole.

Fig. 23. Lad Khan (Surya) temple after conservation, Aihole.

Fig. 24. Kāśī Viśwanātha, Virupāksha and other temples before conservation, Pattadakal.

Fig. 25. Kāśī Viśwanātha, Virupāksha and other temples after conservation.

Fig. 26. Stone replica of *Krishnalīlā* scene from Badami temples, Badami (6th-7th century AD) depicting Krishna stealing butter (*Navanītha chora*).

Fig. 27. Ancient stone statue of Saint-musician, Purandaradāsa, from Hampi excavation.

Fig. 28. Chalukyan architectural features introduced by the author in a modern residential building, Bangalore.

were established, one each at Badami, Aihole and Bagalkot in charge of experienced conservators. Preference was given to repairs to Huchimalli temple, Gaudargudi, Durga temple, Chakragudi, Jaina and Jyotirlinga groups of temples and Ladkhan (Surya) temple. Structural repairs involved strengthening of the sunken foundations and re-setting the dislodged pillars. Replacing cracked lintels and beams and water-tightening the heavily leaking roofs were other measures undertaken. After desilting and repairing an ancient step-well in the village, gardens were laid out in front of Huchappa Gudi and Ladkhan and Durga temples. I must record here my gratitude to my colleagues Srikanthiah, M.M. Raichur, D.B. Krishna and Dharmaiah who devoted all their energy to give a long lease of life to the monuments of Aihole, Pattadakal, Badami, Lakkundi, Hangal, Balligame and Bankapura in Karnataka.

Our excavation at Dwarka on shore in 1979-80 had yielded a pottery, which was similar to the Lustrous Red

Ware found in the excavation at Prabhas, another Mahabharata period port south of Dwarka. This pottery, dating to the 15th century BC, indicated the existence of a mid-second millennium BC site at Dwarka. It appeared that the township which the sea had destroyed and transported its pottery and sediments may be the ancient Dwarka referred to in the *Mausalaparva* of *Mahabharata* (16.7.17)

Fig. 29. Temple of Dwārkādhīsh (13th-15th century), Dwarka. Conservation in progress.

Fig. 30. Vishnu temple of 9th century found below modern building, Dwarka.

according to which Arjuna was warned by Krishna that Dwarka would be swallowed by the sea and that the residents should vacate the city immediately. After they vacated the town, this "golden city of Dwarka was submerged".

7

Discovery of Original Submerged Dwarka

Before undertaking underwater exploration for the first time in India, it was necessary to make sure that the present Dwarka was the site where the ancient Dwarka of Mahabharata tradition was built. In the light of the claim of two other sites in Saurashtra, which some scholars had assumed to be the original (*Mula*) Dwarka, further investigation was necessary. One such site is Mul Dwarka in Una Taluk of Junagadh district. Another site is Madhavpur Ghod situated on the sea, 56 km south-east of Porbandar, and the third claimant for the honour of being Lord Krishna's Dwarka is Visawada (Fig. 33), 40 km south of present Dwarka on way to Porbandar. None of these sites is referred to in ancient texts. Mul Dwarka was excavated by Hirananda Sastry *(Annual Report of the Baroda State Archaeological Department)* in the thirties of the last century, but all that he found was an early historic settlement made at the beginning of the present era. My exploration of Mul Dwarka confirmed his findings. Hence, it had to be ruled out for further exploration. At Madhavpur

Fig. 31. Plinths of Temples I and II below Vishnu temple (III), Dwarka.

Fig. 32. Debris of a township transported by sea action found in Dwarka, onshore excavation.

and Visawada also there is no trace of any settlement earlier than the first few centuries of the present era. Junagadh itself, where there is a hill anciently known as Urjayanta and subsequently renamed Raivataka, could not be considered as Dwarka as there is no sea here, while ancient Dwarka was situated on sea shore with a good harbour.

The high probability of finding the submerged Dwarka in the sea near modern Dwarka increased in view of the clear mention in the *sabha parva* of *Mahabharata* (*Mbh. sabha parva* 13.49 to 52) and the *Vishnu parva* of *Harivamśa* (*Harivamśa-Vishṇu parva*) about the sea near Dwarka. The exact location of Dwarka is given in *Skanda purana* (*Skanda purāṇa*). It says, "Dwarka anciently known as Kusasthali is situated at the confuence of Gomati and western sea."

The modern Dwarka town with its beautiful 13th-15th century temple of Dwarkadhish stands at the confluence

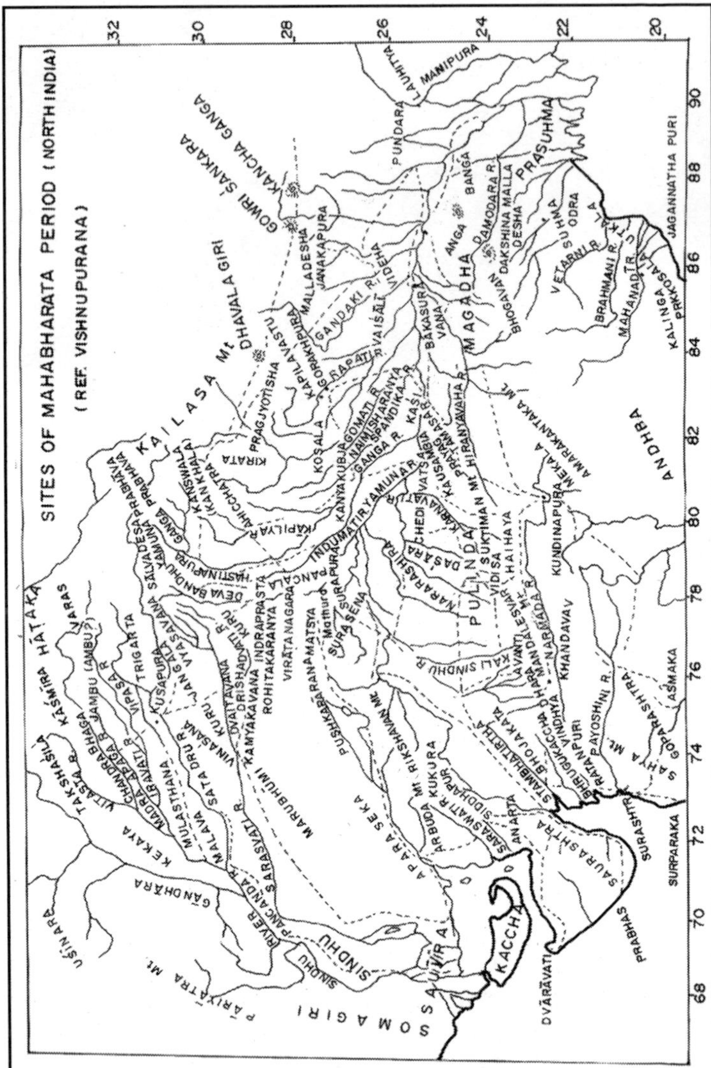

Fig. 33. Map showing sites of Mahābhārata period according to *Vishnu Purana*.

of the River Gomati with the western (Arabian) sea in Okhamandal of Saurashtra. There is also a temple of Kuseswara Mahadev built perhaps in the early centuries of the present era at the entrance to Dwarkadhish temple. But the reference in *Harivamśa* to Kusasthali as surrounded by the sea suggests that it was an island. Elsewhere in *Harivamśa*, it is said that Krishna built a city where once the town of Kusasthali existed and named it Dvārāvatī. The island of Bet Dwarka, 30 km north of mainland Dwarka, is also a holy place associated with the activities of Sri Krishna and his consorts. It was therefore necessary first to explore the Gulf of Kutch where Bet Dwarka is situated and then explore the Arabian Sea bed near modern Dwarka.

Bet Dwarka which is now an island (Fig. 34) was anciently connected by a land bridge with the mainland near Okha and also with *Gopi talav*. It is referred to as Antardvīpa, Kusasthali and Sankhodhara and is famous for its wealth of good quality conch (*śankha*). Shell-working and pearl-fishing were two major industries of ancient Dwarka.

A careful study of the ancient shoreline map of 1880 of Bet Dwarka and the submarine topographical features of the Gulf of Kutch and the near shore region of the Arabian sea at Dwarka had been made by the oceanographers at the NIO. They had observed that from the calcareous sandstone of intertidal origin, it could be concluded that the sea level in the Gulf was as much as 60 m lower ten thousand years ago. Six to thirty metre high pinnacles separated by flat terraces lie submerged in the Gulf. The sea level 3000 years ago must have been 10 to 15 m below the present level exposing some of the hillocks. The *Mahabharata (Sabha parva)* specifically says that at Kusasthali there was the Raivataka hill on one side and the sea on other sides. Presently too, the 30 to 45 m high terraced hill covered by jungle growth and inhabited by wild pigs can

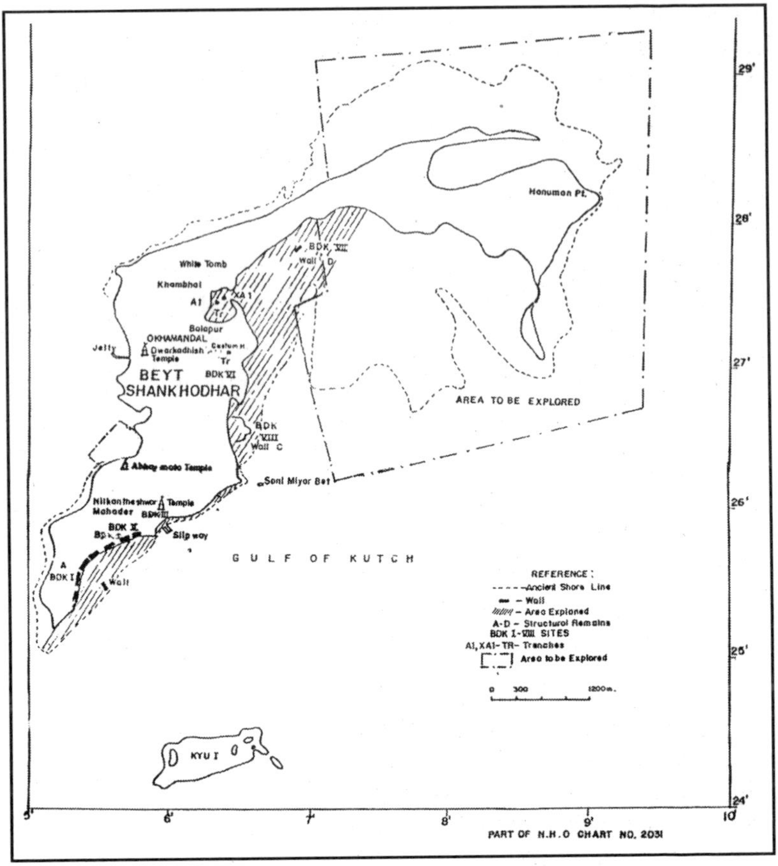

Fig. 34. Explored sites in Bet Dwarka (Shankhodhara).

be seen on the eastern flank of Bet Dwarka, which is rightly identified by Prof. Umashankar Joshi as Kusasthali-*Antardvipa* of *Mahabharata.* It may be recalled here that according to *Harivamsa* the sea was asked by Krishna to yield 12 *yojanas* of land for constructing Dwarka on mainland because the narrow strip of land at the foot of the hill in Bet Dwarka was insufficient for the increasing number of Yadava immigrants from Mathura.

EXCAVATION ON BET DWARKA SHORE

The island of Bet Dwarka (lat. 22° 25″ N, long. 69° 5″ E), anciently known as Kusasthali, and Sankhodhara is said to have been the pleasure resort of Krishna. His consorts Satyabhama and Jambavati are believed to have lived here. According to *Padma Purana,* Vishnu, in his cosmic sleep, found that Sankhasura tried to destroy or steal the *Veda,* and the *Veda* hid itself in the sea. It is then that Vishnu assumed the form of a fish, entered the sea, killed Sankhasura and rescued the *Veda*. The legend is perhaps an allusion to the attack on Kusasthali by the non-vedic Panchajana Rakshasas. On the other hand, the *Gārgya samhitā* says that the great sage Trita who found that his disciple Kakshivahana had cursed him to be in the form of a *śankha* until Sri Krishna restores him to a human form.

PROBLEMS OF ORGANISING THE ARCHAEOLOGICAL CENTRE (MAC)

For a land archaeologist like me, undertaking exploration and excavation in the sea was the greatest challenge especially because I had hardly any experience of excavating in turbulent sea beset with dangerous sea animals and lurking with dangers of current, cyclones and swells. Furthermore, the visibility in the nearshore area of the Arabian Sea is poor because of suspended sediment, making diving and photography very difficult. The divers have to take pictures of submerged objects. To add to these problems, the buildings of ancient Dwarka had survived in bits here and there on the sea bed and are buried under thick layers of sediment and even vegetation. The NIO scientists had studied the offshore area of the sea but not the nearshore area, i.e. two or three kilometers from shore, where we expected remains of the ancient city of Dwarka. More than all, not a single professional archaeologist in India knew diving, and without this important manpower underwater excavation and interpretation would not be scientific. The NIO also had no trained divers. Initially, we took the help of commercial divers but the result was not satisfactory. Hence, we decided to recruit archaeologists and train them in diving, underwater photography, underwater drawing, airlifting the sediments covering buried structures and to prepare the objects for documentation and even video-filming. But the response to our call for applications from the youth to be trained in Marine Archaeology was very poor. Only two applicants came forward and one backed out. Undaunted by this difficulty, we trained the first archaeologist P. Gudigar in diving and other operations with the help of Srinivas Bandodkar, a very competent commercial photographer-cum-diver. He was a great asset to us. In a short period of two years he could train five archaeologists and two NIO photographers. The next problem we had to face was procuring diving equipment, underwater video and still cameras, survey instruments, airlifts, generators and metal detectors. Gradually we purchased them. The NIO scientists and directors were always helpful in our research. Initially, the INSA gave us seed money but we had to wait for a couple of years to get funds from DST and CSIR. No doubt Marine Archaeological Research is quite expensive. Even after ten years (1981 to 1991), we could not procure GPS (Global Positioning System) to locate our targets, and underwater communication system. We could not get a modern vessel specially built for marine archaeology. We could hire only local motorised fishing vessels and small *hodis.* Among other problems, mention may be made of trouble from ill-informed officials.

Before launching offshore exploration, we had obtained permission from the customs authority at Okha to carry out diving and other operations in Dwarka and Bet Dwarka waters and to carry the necessary scientific instruments and cameras as per a list given by us to the customs officer. On 23 December 1983, I was waiting near Rupen Bandar for the trawler operated by Muhammad to take the exploration party to Dwarka waters. A scare-crow-like looking person approached me and asked whether I was waiting for a boat to bring *māl*, by which he meant 'smuggled goods'. I brushed him aside saying ours is a government party exploring submerged Dwarka waters near S.N. temple. Suddenly we found a speed boat approaching our boat. The crew were in khaki uniform, and one of the members on the boat had a gun pointed towards our boat. The speed boat ran amock dashing against our boat when one of the divers was about to dive. Soon we could recognise the gun-trotter as a customs official. He asked me whether I had obtained the necessary permit. I replied, "yes". "Show me," he demanded. I coolly replied, "It is in my camp office." When further questioned what we are looking for here, I had to bluntly say, "for ancient stone structures of Dwarka." I made it clear that we were scientists of NIO and the customs office at Okha had given us a permit. He had been misinformed by the his agent that we were searching for gold ingots dropped by smugglers. After finding that we were genuine scientists, he went back. Had our diver dived when the customs boat came near our boat, he would have been shot by customs people as per rules. But Muhammad knew the rules and asked the diver not to dive.

Another incident which we were about to face in Dwarka waters was when one of the divers was about to dive. In spite of instructions from the port authority at our request, directing fisherman not to run their boats within 1 km from Dwarka shore to avoid damage or loss of the marker buoys laid by us, one fisherman was found spreading his net in the prohibited area. Our crew started shouting at him, but he brought his boat and showed us a shark caught in the net. We then realised that if he had not spread his net, the shark would have attacked our divers. We expressed our gratitude to him. Normally sharks do not come to shallow waters. Perhaps this shark was stranded in low tide. This is one of the instances cited to highlight the danger to be faced by explorers.

The sea is unpredictable. Several times it had become choppy in the afternoon when we were on the high sea. Sailing in a small fiberglass or wooden *hodi* from the mother ship to the shore exposes us to the risk of the boat capsizing even in shallow waters.

To add to these difficulties, we had woefully inadequate funds with the result that we could not work in the sea for more than 40 to 50 days in a year. That was from December to February. But the commitment on the part of all members of the undersea search team to put in their best effort has yielded astonishing results when the staff strength (six) and limited funds (about eight lakhs of rupees per year) are taken into account. During operations in the sea, we had to face many dangers due to the storms and from poisonous sea organisms. Recently the marine archaeologists had to face the gun-trotting naxalites on the east coast. These terrorists took away very expensive cameras, GPS, communication system and even generators. It is only since 1998 that underwater communication system advanced survey system and GP3 were purchased.

Objective

The primary objective of marine archaeology in general is to explore, excavate and preserve historical shipwrecks and submerged ports, which constitute the cultural heritage of man. Marine archaeology in India has a two-fold objective of shedding light on maritime activity in the so-called 'Dark Age' of Indian history and to reconstruct its maritime history. It can generate scientific data necessary for determining the sea level fluctuation during the last 5000 years. For filling up the gap in Indian history between the end of the Indus civilisation (1700 BC) and the beginning of the Buddhist period (450 BC), literary evidence had to be supported by archaeological evidence from excavations of cities of Dwarka. India has perhaps the richest cultural heritage under the sea by way of both shipwrecks and submerged ports such as Dwarka, Prabhas (Somanath), Khambhat, Bhrugukaccha (Broach), Surparaka (Sopara), Gharapuri (in Elephanta Island), Udyavara (near Malpe), Muziris (Cranganore), Rameswaram, Poompuhar, and Kalingaptna. This heritage should be explored and preserved. The ICUCH has adopted a convention for preservation of underwater cultural heritage.

As a member I participated in the drafting of the convention by the ICOMOS International Committee on Underwater Cultural Heritage (ICUCH).

LOCATION OF DWARKA

The earliest epigraphical reference to Dwarka of the early historical period as a seat of Śrī Krishṇa in Okha is contained in the Pāliṭhāṇa copper-plate grant of Sāmanta Siṁhāditya of Garulaka family dated to AD 574 (*Epigraphia Indica,* Vol. XI, 18, 11-12). The association of the Ujjayanta hill of Girnar (Junagadh) with the Raivataka hill of ancient Dwarka by some scholars does not appear to be convincing. According to H.G. Sastri, "The Raivataka hill lay in the vicinity of Dwarka (which was submerged)." The name 'Raivataka' did not denote Girnar in early times. The latter was known as Urjayat or Ujjayanta. The Jaina *Āgama* works locate the *dīkshā* of Arishṭanemi near Dvārāvatī, and his *Kaivalya* and *Nirvāṇa* on Ujjayanta. According to H.G. Sastri, long after the original Raivataka hill became extinct along with original Dwarka, its name was applied to the hill behind the Damodara temple at Junagadh.

The *Skanda Purāṇa* locates Ujjayanta to the west of Bhavanātha temple and the Raivataka hill near the temple of Dāmodara. In course of time, however, the two names became synonymous and Girnar came to be called Raivataka. But by no stretch of imagination Girnar can be considered original Dwarka in view of the fact that there is no sea nearby. Original Dwarka was founded near or at the foot of the hillock Raivataka (Sastri, H.G., 1988, 63-64).

Archaeological evidence proves that the hill on the eastern fringe of Bet Dwarka was Raivataka and the original settlement of the late Harappan period discovered here as a result of offshore and onshore exploration by the Marine Archaeology Centre represents Kuśasthalī where a new town was built and named Dwarka (Shastree, K.K., 1988, 25). There are several pinnacles and terraces submerged in the Gulf of Kutch (Hashimi, N.H. *et. al.*, 1978, 1-7) and they too might have been known as Raivataka before submersion (Fig. 20).

There is a mention of Śrī Krishṇa as 'Lord of Dwarka' in the 6th century inscription of Siṁhāditya. The establishment of Śāradāpīṭha by Ādi Śankara in the beginning of the 9th century and the visit of the Pratihara Emperor, Nāgabhaṭa II of Kanauj to holy Dwarka and Piṇḍatāraka *kshetras* in the first half of the 9th century confirm that the reference is to mainland Dwarka. The *Tīrthakalpataru* of Lakshmīdāsa (written in the first quarter of 12th century) mentions Dwarka identified with the modern settlements at Dwarka and Bet Dwarka.

Excavations in Bet Dwarka

Hirananda Sastry, director of archaeology, Baroda, who excavated near Nilakantha Mahadev temple in Bet Dwarka came across a potsherd inscribed *nandasa* (of nanda) in Brahmi script of 2nd century AD. A survey of the island by me revealed habitations of the protohistoric as well as early historic periods all along the east coast but ancient stone walls were however heavily damaged at intervals by spring tides and local people. We could identify four sectors of the protohistoric settlements on the basis of pottery and structural remains on the shore and in the sea bed. At the southern end is the site designated by us as BDK I-II; the central sector as BDK-VIII, the northern sector as BDK VII and the fourth one near Nilakantha Mahadev temple where four rock-cut wells overgrown with jungle are still visible, as BDK III-IV.

MARINE ARCHAEOLOGICAL EXPEDITIONS

In the course of the first marine archaeological expedition in April 1983, a heavily disturbed rubble wall came to light in the upper terrace at the sites designated as BDK I-II Siddi Bawa Pir on the southern shore. This was exposed by careful excavation (Fig. 35). Besides shell objects, a distinct pottery of Lustrous Red Ware (LRW) fabric and types was found in the section of the protohistoric wall, behind which a later wall also yielded pottery of early historic period. Both were sent for TL dating at the Physical Research Laboratory, Ahmedabad. The LRW was dated 1528 BC and the early historic pottery is dated 1st century AD. This evidence suggested that here existed a township at least 3500 years old, but what was more important was to find the submerged part of ancient Dwarka. Hence, the second expedition (1984) concentrated on underwater exploration and excavation. Initially we had to engage country fishing boats and commercial divers. Subsequently, qualified archaeologists like P. Gudigar, Sila Tripathi, A.S. Gaur and Sundaresh took to diving, excavation and airlifting the sediments covering buried structures, which were later photographed. In subsequent expeditions, a young lady diver by the name Manavi Thakkar, trained abroad in underwater exploration and photography, was employed. All the time Srinivas Bandodkar supervised the diving operations.

Fig. 35. Rubble wall on middle terrace of eastern shore in Bet Dwarka (site BDK II).

As a result of sustained diving in BDK I-II, we could locate another wall of large dressed blocks of sandstone built on the wave-cut bench in lower terrace in the intertidal zone. It lies submerged in flow tide. According to B.U. Nayak, Head of the Ocean Engineering Division of NIO, who actively participated in three expeditions in Bet Dwarka and Dwarka, the dressed blocks of stone in situ are too heavy to be moved by waves and currents. The rubble scattered all over indicated extensive destruction of houses built of smaller blocks. Controlled diving and excavation in sea bed were made possible by the use of a caisson, a steel box without bottom or top, in which airlifting was done. The airlift works like a suction pump and brings water-mixed sediment, etc. to the sieve kept in the boat where potsherds, shell bangles, beads, etc. are collected. In the course of the second expedition, fourteen cruises to Dwarka and eleven to Bet Dwarka were undertaken from Rupen.

In Trench No. UW 6 (Fig. 36) sunk 400 m seaward of BDK II up to 3.50 m water depth, yielded a unique seal of conch shell engraved with the motif of a composite animal of bull, unicorn and goat (Fig. 37). It was recovered while examining the sediment in the sieve. This three-headed animal resembles the figures on Bahrain seals datable to 18th-17th century BC, if not slightly earlier. The mention of the use of seal by Dwarka citizens in the *Harivamsa* and our discovery of the seal confirm that ancient Dwarka existed here in 18th-17th century BC. Another important find from the intertidal zone of Bet Dwarka is the upper part of a votive trough-like earthen vessel inscribed with seven letters in the Late Harappan cursive script which is further evolved and written from left to right (Fig. 38). The inscription reads *ma-ha-ha-gach-sh-ha-pā (Fig. 38) Mahāhagacha (mahākacha) shah-pa* conveying the sense, sea (*mahākaccha*), Lord (*Shah*), and protect (*pā*). A sailor or merchant must have made an offering in this vessel to the sea god (Varuṇa) for seeking his protection (for further details, see Rao, S.R., 1999, p. 115ff.). In this connection, attention may be drawn to a terracotta sealing from G.F. Dales' excavation at Mohenjodaro, on which a boat with a cabin, an oar and two birds perching on the edge of the vessel are depicted. The inscription above the boat written in Indus cursive script reads *pak tras āp pār = pāk – tras – āp – pār* conveying the sense, guard (*pak* – guardian), of turbulent (*tras*), water (*āp*), and save (*pār*). It is an appeal to the guardian of the turbulent water (Varuna, the sea god) to save (the boat and men). The birds are the shore-finding birds *(diśākāka)* used by sailors to lead them to the shore. The *Arthaśāstra* of 3rd century BC refers to *diśākākas.*

The inscription on the votive jar of Bet Dwarka can be assigned to the 17th century BC. It is the forerunner of the Brahmi script evolved from late Harappan script. Not far from BDK II are two rock-cut slipways extending from the

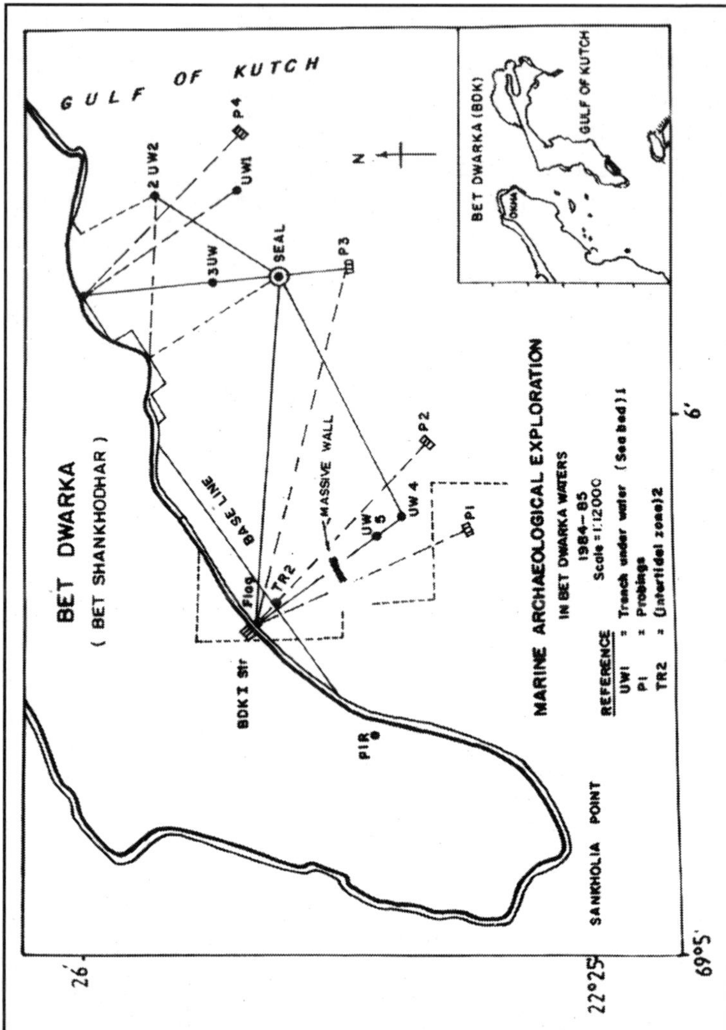

Fig. 36. Findspot of seal in (Trench UW6) in Bet Dwarka.

Fig. 37. Seal with a composite figure of bull, unicorn and goat, Bet Dwarka.

rocky beach into the intertidal zone. The sloping floor of the slipways must have been cut and dressed manually for launching boats. Some weathering effect and denudation, which are natural in the interitidal zone according to Dr. Nayak, are also noticeable. The varying width of 4 m and 6 m of the ramps suggests that they were meant for

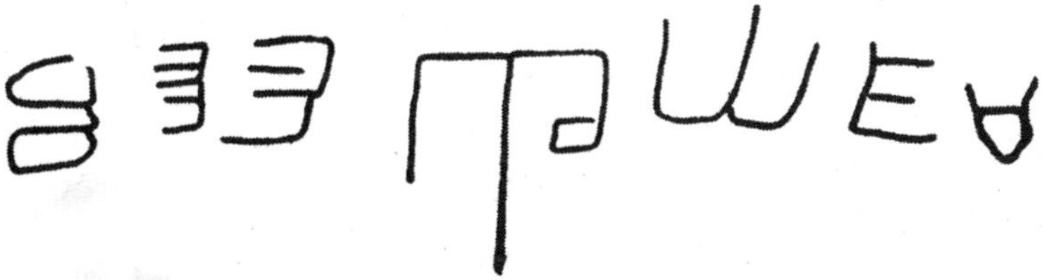

Reading: *ma hā ha gach sh-h-pā = mahhā (mahā) gacha (Kacha) shah-Pā*
Inscribed part of an earthen Vessel

Fig. 38. Inscription of Late Indus script reading *mahhā-gacha-shah-pā*, Bet Dwarka.

Fig. 39. A massive wall of large stone blocks in BDK VII.

launching boats of varying sizes. During the third expedition in 1985, seventeen cruises were made from Rupen to Dwarka although there is no jetty at either place. In Rupen hundreds of fishing trawlers are beached and a few are anchored in low water. Two cruises were made to Bet Dwarka from Okha. A massive wall of large blocks of stone was discovered and cleared for photograph in lowest ebb tide in BDK VII, north of Balapur bay (Fig. 39). These blocks are laid in five regular courses covered by sea organisms (Fig. 39). A comparative study of the shoreline of Bet Dwarka Revenue map of 1880 and latest hydrographic survey map shows that the coastal indentations of 1880 have been smoothened out by the action of waves and currents. A small bay formation is also taking place between the southern promontory (near custom house) and northern promontory (near Dargah Pir) in Balapur shoreline. This crenulated bay provides good shelter to country crafts during monsoon. The vast mud flat extending over 1 km in the intertidal zone and fully exposed in ebb tide was part of ancient Kusasthali Dwarka as is clear from the late Harappan pottery types such as perforated jar and flanged dish. The lower terrace also formed part of ancient Dwarka settlement later which yielded similar pottery from two trenches (BDK VII) sunk here. The upper terraces were however, occupied in the early historic and medieval periods. The Red Polished Ware datable to 1st to 4th century AD serves as a datum line. During the Fifth Expedition (1986) between the southern protohistoric settlements in BDK I-II and the Balapur Bay settlements in the north (BDK VI-VII), an extensive fortification wall, 558 m in peripheral length, (Fig. 40) was discovered and the site was designated as BDK VIII. Trenches were laid on either side of the wall and eight courses of masonry were traced. This enclosure wall built on wave-cut bench must have served as a fortification wall for important buildings within it, but they are all levelled

Fig. 40. Fortification wall (558 m long) exposed in low tide, BDK VIII.

Fig. 41. Stone mould, bead, pottery and shell artefacts from underwater excavation, Bet Dwarka.

up by waves and currents. The fort wall, extant up to 1.5 m height, must have been much higher. The protohistoric pottery found in the trenches here provides the clue to its construction in the same period as the wall in BDK I-II. The ancient Kusasthali Dwarka must have extended all along the eastern coast from Siddi Bawa Pir to Balapur and further north covering a distance of 4 km. Underwater excavation by NIO (1996-97) near the modern jetty of Bet Dwarka yielded a few protohistoric potsherds and triangular stone anchors with three holes for fixing wooden stakes in them. It is, therefore, obvious that the southern shore served as a berthing place for ships of ancient Dwarka. Among other significant finds from Bet Dwarka intertidal zone mention may be made of a stone mould for casting spearheads (Fig. 41), perforated jar and shell beads and bangles and a copper fish-hook of 18th century BC, which form antiquities of submerged Dwarka.

DWARKA ON THE ARABIAN SEA

Underwater exploration of submerged Dwarka (Fig. 42) was started in 1984 about 100 m seaward of the temple of Samudranarayana (SN) at the mouth of Gomati River (Fig. 43). Further seaward, about 200 m from SN, stray blocks of sandstone used in masonry were found. In deep water survey during the third and fourth expeditions

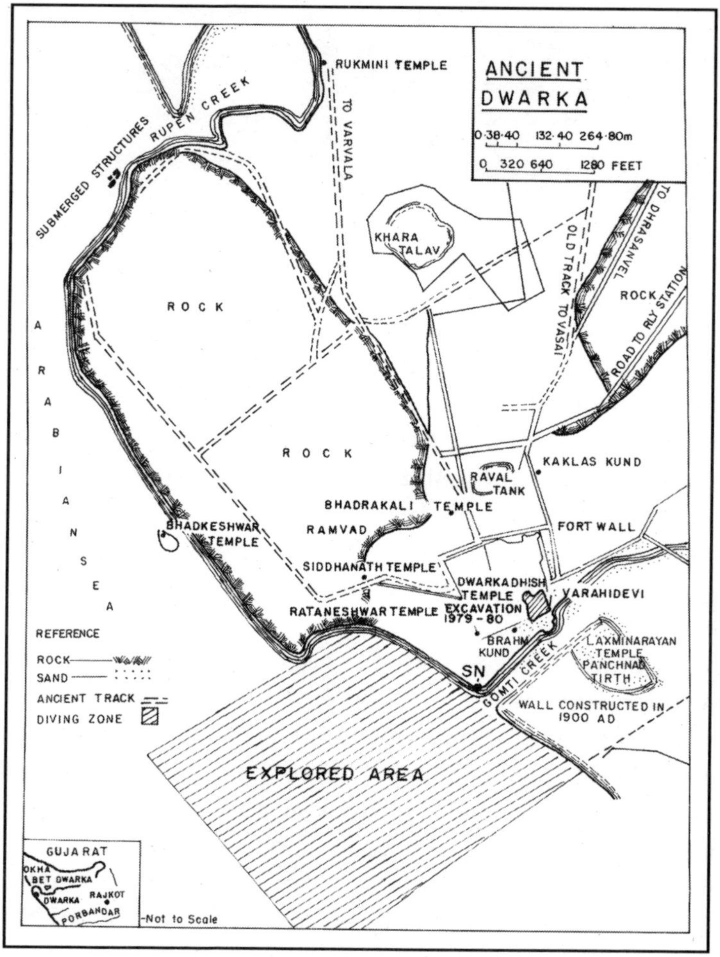

Fig. 42. 'Ancient Dwarka' – Site plan of excavation onshore.

Fig. 43. Samudranarayana and Dwarakadhish temples overlooking the Arabian Sea.

(1985-86), several triangular stone anchors datable to 15th-16th century BC were recovered. They are similar in shape and size to those used in 14th-13th century BC at Kition, a Bronze Age site in Cyprus (Honor Frost, 1973, p. 400). Two heavily damaged structures were discovered in 6 m water depth on the transit line extending from Dwarkadhish-Samudranarayana temple towers up to 600 m seaward. The nearshore structures may be assigned to 1st-4th century AD. On December 8, a bastion, circular in shape, built of large dressed sandstone blocks on a boulder foundation in the sea at buoy No. 35 was documented after removing vegetation and concretions covering it. The submerged palaeo channel of Gomati, on the banks of which ancient Dwarka was built, was also recorded. On 13 December 1986, the sea became choppy with 5 to 6 m high breakers. Hence work had to be suspended for a couple of days. On 20 December our research vessel *Vedhavati* had a miraculous escape on its way to Okha, when it struck a sand bank in just 2.5 m water depth about 10 km from

Fig. 44. Circular bastion of the fortification of submerged Dwarka.

Okha. The sea was rough and current strong but somehow the vessel could be saved. On our return journey, the channel between two sandbanks shown in the chart was followed. The country boat *Rāmbān* carrying expensive instruments anchored at Rupen was smashed to a rock in a cyclone on the night of 11 October 1987. It was damaged but as if by miracle the costly instruments were safe. This news reached me on the 12 morning at Jamnagar where the first marine archaeology conference was being inaugurated by Sri R. Balakrishna, chief secretary to the government of Gujarat.

The findings of the first five expeditions were discussed at the Conference attended by Alexander Flinders, founder member of the British Maritime Archaeological Society and other scientists from India. Undaunted by the mishap of *Rāmbān,* we resumed underwater exploration deploying *Vedhavati* and another vessel.

The sixth expedition in 1988 yielded very important results. We engaged two vessels, *Vedhavati* (Fig. 44) as well as *Ghelano Madad*, in December 1988. Two bastions, a huge wall and parts of a third bastion were exposed in airlift operation. They were manually cleared of vegetation growth and finally plotted by diver-draftsmen. With the acquisition of an underwater Osprey TV camera, video coverage was made by Bandodkar under the direction of Vision India. The editing and surface shooting were entrusted to Sambamurthy, Advani and Ravindra of 'Vision India'. In December the sea is normally calm and the swells are rare, but on 21st December the sea was very choppy and *Vedhavati* was rolling heavily. A little later, 1 km seaward of SN, it was possible to airlift sediments in trenches and reveal the continuity of Gomati palaeo-channel in 8 m depth near buoy 54.

During the seventh expedition (January 1989), the fortification walls built of large dressed sandstone blocks and studded with circular (Fig. 45) and semi-circular bastions were laid bare on both the banks of the

Fig. 45. *Vedhavati* research vessel.

palaeo-channel of Gomati. A large door socket of stone with a hole was found in situ at the entrance to a massive fort wall in 5.5 m water depth. There lay a triangular stone anchor in the submerged channel nearby. In rough sea also we had to ferry between Gomati *ghat* and the mother ship *(Vedhavati)* anchored at 1 km distance or more. The small motorised boat *Indira* was later toppled by high waves. Despite bad weather photographs of submerged buildings were taken (Figs. 46-47).

GEOPHYSICAL SURVEY IN DWARKA WATERS
(Dec. 1989 to Jan. 1990)

The ninth expedition in 1989-90 brought to light several important buildings as a result of the application of geophysical survey techniques by the NIO team headed by K.H. Vora, which deployed side-scan sonar, echosounder and sub-bottom profiler. The echo sounder gives the depths

Fig. 46. Submerged wall of ancient Dwarka.

Fig. 47. Another submerged wall of ancient Dwarka.

and sea-bed contours, while the side scan sonar provides a plan view of the sea floor. The topographical and lithological variations on the sea-bed are recorded on sonographs in the form of tonal variations. The system comprises of image processing side-scan recorder, the tow fish and interconnecting cable. The transducers fixed on either side of the tow fish cable can scan 25 to 500 m on both sides of the survey track. The system being microprocessorised corrects for speed and slant range. For purposes of position-fixing of objects found in sea-bed Mini Ranger III was used (for details see Rao, 1999). In subsequent surveys, the GPS (Global Positioning System) was used for position fixing. The objects indicated on sonograph during geophysical survey were physically examined, cleaned and photographed by diver archaeologists. Three walls built of large stone blocks and a bastion built with lunate-shaped stones and held together by L-shaped joints were documented. Two houses are partly traced within the fortifications on the northern bank of the submerged palaeo channel of Gomati. Prismatic and triangular stone anchors lying in the channel suggest that small boats used to ferry passengers and cargo between the harbour and warehouses. A long wall of a hall was traced up to 7 m length. On the whole, four enclosures on the right bank and one on the left could be identified. The survey conducted in 2 to 22 m water depth in December 1989 comprised of 130-1 km of echo sounding, side-scan sonar survey and shallow seismic profiling, the map scale being 1:1500. The area covered extended from Rupen port to Dwarka lighthouse and further south up to the wall built by erstwhile Baroda state. The survey revealed the ancient Gomati channel, 400 m wide, up to 1.5 km in the northeast-southwest direction. Besides the drainage system, submerged geomorphic features such as scarps and terraces were also recorded. The submerged Gomati channel is in the same direction as that of its channel on land. It is

Fig. 48. Diver-Scientist Manavi Thakkar surveying ancient Dwarka with the help of underwater scooter.

V-shaped near the shore and becomes wider and shallower offshore. The two banks of Gomati are clearly seen in easternmost lines and the flanks have a steep gradient. The nearshore area is uneven, the middle part rugged due to presence of structures and the offshore is even. During this expedition Miss Manavi Thakkar surveyed submerged buildings deploying underwater scooter (Fig. 48).

TWELFTH EXPEDITION (December 1991-January 1992)

We had as our objective of this expedition the demarcation of the limits of the anciently submerged city of Dwarka built on the banks of the palaeo-channel of Gomati and to document all structures and also to trace the berthing facility for sea sailing vessels noticed at the scarp-like feature in 10-12 m water depth. For supply of air to divers, both SDDE and SCUBA systems were used. The newly acquired Aquazepp, an underwater scooter, was useful for rapid survey. Mostly, Manavi Thakkar and Srinivas Bandodkar operated it. It is necessary to mention here that offshore operations being very expensive, they had to be limited to 15 days in Dwarka waters and 5 days in Somnath waters. The funds available were extremely meagre each year. If adequate funds, say Rs. 25 to 30 lakhs, were provided every year for field operations only, much more work could have been done in fewer number of expeditions which would be more economical and preliminary offshore operations could have been reduced.

A steel-hulled vessel MFV *Penta* owned by Mr. Bernard was hired from 27 December 1991 to 27 January 1992. The positions of the boat and buoys at Dwarka were fixed in stationary condition by taking sextant angles of three suitable shore objects, e.g., Dwarkadhish temple tower, Samudranarayana temple tower and light house. The total area surveyed and explored was divided into eight zones. Loose dressed stone blocks used in the construction, a few walls in situ up to 3 or 4 courses and bastions were discovered and documented. In zone 2, more than 20 semi-circular blocks of bastions and hundreds of loose dressed stones used in the masonry of houses, bastions and fortifications were noticed. In zone 3 prismatic and triangular stone anchors were found. In zone 4 a rocky ridge, 1 to 1.5 m high and about 30 m long, was noticed. Near the ridge was lying a large anchor. A circular stone door socket was found near the gateway of the submerged fort in zone 6. The massive stones used in the construction of fort walls were too heavy to be transported by currents, but the upper courses have collapsed leaving only 2 or 3 courses in situ, both in the case of walls and bastions. Drawings of all structures submerged are prepared (Fig. 49). Only two bastions were entirely intact. The structures south of transit line served as protection walls of the city. The site plan of ancient submerged Dwarka (Fig. 50) and artist's view (Fig. 51) give an idea of the location of the harbour and city.

Fig. 49. A large submerged wall of ancient Dwarka.

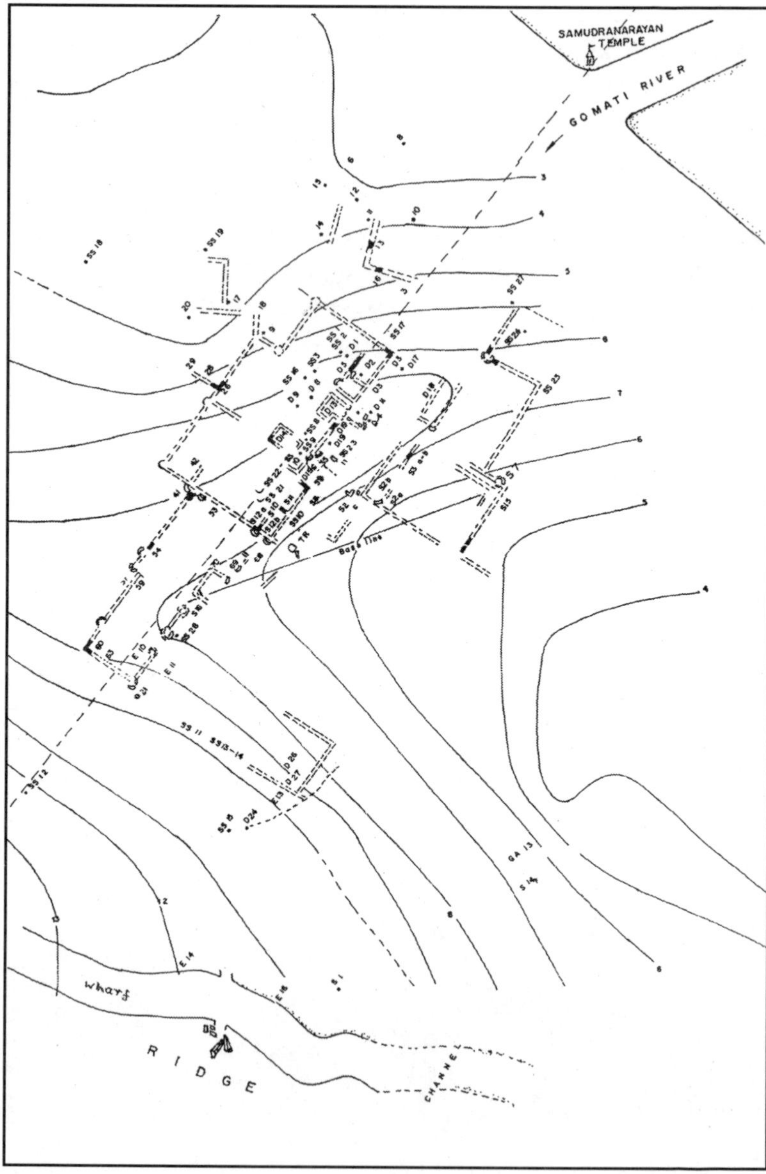

Fig. 50. Contour plan of submerged towship and harbour of Dwarka on Gomati channel.

Fig. 51. Artists' view of submerged Dwarka port town.

A Day to Remember (from My Personal Diary)

07-01-1992: On return from Somnath previous night at 10 p.m. I was tired because of the strenuous 700 km long road journey by taxi. But I woke up at 6 a.m. and after a bath and short visit to the temple for *darsan* of Lord Sri Krishna at 7.30 a.m., I had breakfast at 8 a.m. and left for Gomatighat. On the way I saw the road unusually clean and wet and thought there was drizzle last night. Vora and I entered the small boat (*Dolphin*) at 9 a.m.. As it moved I could see the swell and waves high, while during the 6 previous days the sea was calm. Rolling and pitching, the *Dolphin* took us to *Penta* (the mother boat) anchored 1 km seaward. Sila and Khan dived and reported poor visibility and strong current. So did Gudigar. Sila and Gaur dived again. Conditions became worse at 11 a.m.. By 12 noon, the sea was choppy, waves 2 m high near *Penta* and heavy breakers near SN (Samudranarayana temple on shore). Vora who had gone to shore returned and reported sailing on rough sea was posing a problem. After lunch, around 2.35 p.m., *Dolphin* was ready to take us to the shore after Bandodkar felt that sea would be rougher and reaching shore may become impossible later. We had no clothes to stay on the boat for the night, and arrangements had to be made on shore for Dr. Desai's visit to Dwarkadhish and to *Penta*.

As we (including Vora, Gudigar and Chitare) were 200 m away from SN, the engine of *Dolphin* failed. The breakers, 5 m high, were battering near SN, and entering Gomati channel seemed impossible. However, the driver restarted the engine, skilfully steered the *Dolphin* a few metres back, ran parallel to a low wave and raced towards the channel even as the next wave, 5 m high, behind us came so swiftly and dashed against *Dolphin* that it reeled and fell on side but did not capsize. Fortunately it could avoid the rocks near SN. Thank God! Bernard who was watching on shore was greatly worried about our safety. I had not lost courage although I knew Vora did not know swimming, but Gudigar and Chitare were frightened. Somehow as we reached Gomati steps, Bernard felt relieved. He said to me, "Sir, because of your presence, all were saved." I laughed within myself and said, " It is Lord Krishna's and Lord Somnath's grace which saved us." The *Dolphin* speeded back to the *Penta* and within less than 30 minutes we saw from Gomati ghat *Dolphin* was coming towards SN as the waves appeared smoothened. I somehow had a lurking fear that all was not well. Lo! within a minute or two *Dolphin* avoided a high wave, crossed the next, but was struck by another and was thrown overboard with all crew into the ghastly sea about 50 m northwest of SN; all were trapped under *Dolphin* which for a moment appeared to form the lid of a water coffin for all its occupants (Bandodkar, Sila, Gaur, Sundaresh, Tippu, etc.). I ran to the scene, so did Chitare. Fortunately Sundaresh and Sirsath ran to shore, while Sila, Gaur and Bandodkar lifted *Dolphin* and came out of the trap. Someone shouted Tippu is gone (dead). We knew Tippu (a young operator of the heavy compressor on *Penta*) did not know swimming. Sila rushed to help Bandodkar and others to extricate Tippu while heavy battering of waves was going on. It appears all the crew were thrown out head-down and legs up when *Dolphin* was toppled. But Tippu, as strictly instructed by Bandodkar, clung firmly to his ring life jacket and gradually drifted to the shore safely. Sila, however, caught in the rock-cut channel, was struggling and Sirsath brought him to the shore and I helped Gaur to reach the beach. Tippu was exhausted. Sila was slightly injured and given first-aid. *Dolphin* and its engine were damaged but all the men and crew were saved. As I had crossed 5 to 6 m high waves safely in a dingy a year ago, I was not afraid of high waves, although on another occasion, Pirkhan's dingy had capsized here. In Tranquebar water on east coast, the dingy had capsized while on high sea and thrown out a crew member. On yet another occasion the generator had caught fire and with great presence of mind, the scientist T.C.S. Rao threw away the generator into the sea to avoid the ship from catching fire.

That the residents of Dwarka were literate is obvious from two inscriptions found in Bet Dwarka. They were good sailors and their ships must have reached Bahrain and other ports in the Arabian Gulf. The Bet Dwarka seal depicting bull, unicorn and goat is reminiscent of Bahrain seal. Pearl-fishing was an important industry of Bet Dwarka which is also known as Sankhodhara because of the profusion of good quality *sankha* (conch shells) found in the sea and used as a substitute for metals. That the iron technology was known to the smiths of Dwarka is proved by iron nails found along with protohistoric pottery. A stone mould for casting spearheads suggests manufacture and use of weapons of war recovered from Kusasthali Dwarka. Some parts of a miniature two-wheeled chariot made of brass were also found in Dwarka waters. Its frame is similar to that of the bronze chariot of Daimabad of mid-second millenium BC.

Date of Dvārakā

The first town of Kusasthali built by Kakudmin Raivata, who was a Yadava, had suffered damage for reasons not known. It was rebuilt as the first terraced town of Dwarka by the Yadavas under Krishna's direction. Four rock-cut wells were dug here in upper terrace near Sankhanarayana temple for providing potable water for the residents in protohistoric period. The second town of Dwarka which was built on the mainland was well planned and divided into four or more sectors. They were approachable from land and sea. It is this port town fortified by walls and having 30 to 50 bastions and balcony openings which is described in *Harivamsa Vishnu Parva*, 86. Besides enclosures a couple of roads and drains have been traced. Both the Dwarkas built within a short period of 20 or 30 years were submerged in circa 1600 BC or slightly earlier. This date has been arrived at on the basis of the TL date of pottery from the surviving rubble wall onshore in the middle terrace of BDK II as well as the Late Indus type, inscriptions and fish-hooks referred to earlier. But the buildings on the lower terrace in BDK II must have been built earlier. The total life span of both the Dwarkas was about 100 years. The late Harappan pottery, the Late Indus type seal and epigraphs from Kusasthali Dwarka suggest 17th-18th century BC date. The possibility of finding earlier antiquities if excavation is undertaken in Balapur mud-flats cannot be ruled out. The traditional date of 3102 BC for *Kaliyuga* mentioned in Aihole inscription is contradicted by Hissa Barole inscription. One thing that is certain is the author of the later text *Skanda Purana* seems to have confused Dwarka on the mainland with Kusasthali Dwarka in the island.

Dwarka as an Underwater Museum

A project proposal for the preservation of submerged Dwarka in situ and providing access to visitors has been submitted to the department of culture of the Government of India.

The following conservation measures are necessary to preserve Dwarka, as a unique underwater cultural heritage of man. Apart from its archaeological and historical importance, Dwarka associated with the legendary hero Krishna has great emotional importance.

STAGE I: In the first stage the structures covered by sediment and vegetation should be identified and exposed to view by airlifting and cleaning by the Marine Archaeology Centre of NIO which is fully equipped for the purpose. This work should be done in consultation with

S.R. Rao who directed all the twelve expeditiors. One ROV (submersible), two barge-mounted cranes, two trawlers and two small speed boats may be hired along with the services of twenty commercial divers for about 100 working days. (December to March). The total number of working days will be 200 for uncovering buildings recently covered by sediment and vegetation.

STAGE II: When the structures are being exposed and cleaned, simultaneous conservation work should be undertaken. This involves providing proper foundation to exposed structures, building a coffer dam, resetting fallen architectural members as per drawings already prepared, and raising the height of a few walls, up to 1-5 to 2 m. It is also necessary to provide links in gaps between walls created anciently by the scouring action of the sea. After due experiments, appropriate water grouts and mortar will have to be used for securing the structural cohesion and stability. This work can be executed by an expert body of engineers. It is a technical job involving employment of a large number of commercial divers and use of barge-mounted cranes and heavy airlifts. Both the items can be completed in two seasons of four months each if full use of the fair season (December to March) is made. Instead of building a jetty for landing, a decommissioned submarine may be used.

STAGE III: Providing access to the submerged city in Dwarka water in the fair season for visitors to view can be thought of by providing underwater acrelic tubes or viewing chambers at specific points, as is done in Singapore and Auckland. If these are considered risky, tourists can view the submerged buildings in the monitor kept on boat when underwater video-cameras operate. An additional attraction should be a cruise from Dwarka to Bet Dwarka to see structures exposed in the intertidal zone in ebb tide. Unfortunately the so-called expert from Australia consulted

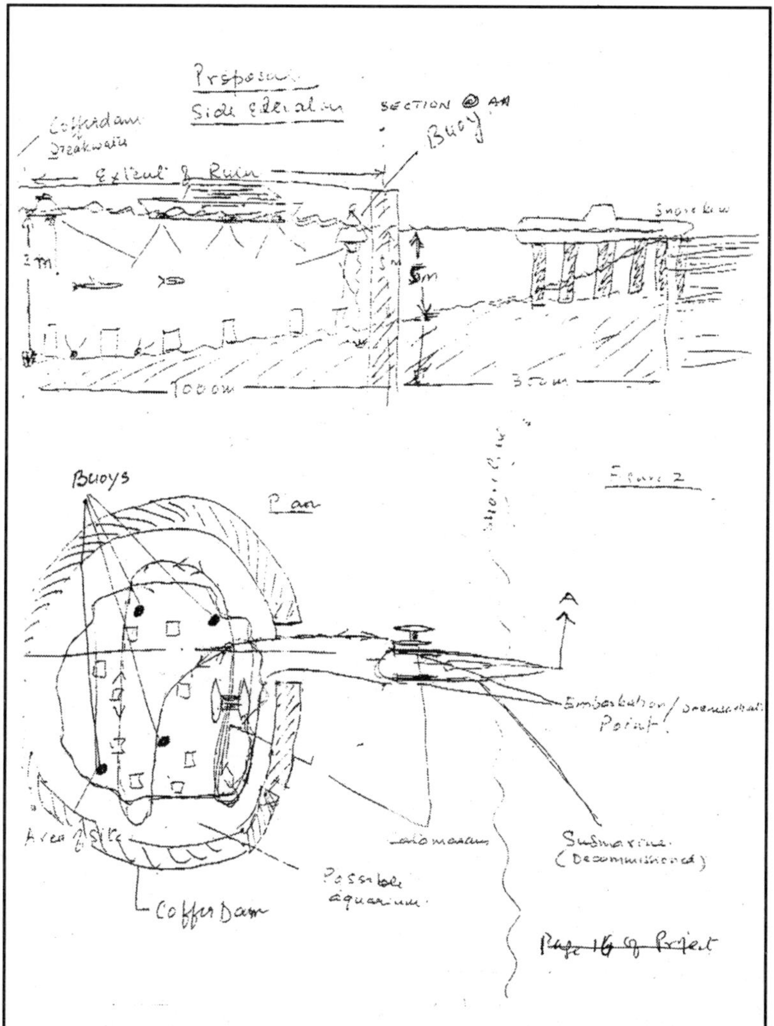

Fig. 52. Sketch plan of the cofferdam and decommissioned submarine (proposed for conservation of submerged Dwarka).

by Gujarat Tourism Department was only a film producer and not a marine engineer. His views are not relevant to our needs. It is suggested by a naval officer that instead of building a jetty at Dwarka, a decommissioned submarine can be used for embarking of tourist (Fig. 53).

Maritime Museum

A maritime museum of antiquities found in excavations at Dwarka, Bet Dwarka, Somnath and Nageswar and diaromas of Lothal port and Dwarka city supplemented by video-films of underwater exploration could be other attractions to visitors.

The *Bhāgavata Purāṇa* and *Harivamśa* mention that Krishna sent a message to Arjuna saying that Dwarka would be submerged by the sea and before the calamity overtook it, the city should be vacated. As the residents went on vacating the city, the sea entered the town and swallowed all buildings except the *Bhagavadālaya* (the mansion of God). The ancient city at the Gomati mouth must have extended further east of Dwarkadhish temple up to the channel along the ridge near the present bus stand. The description of the city given in *Sabhā Parva* of *Mahābhārata* seems to be an exaggeration because Dwarka could not have been 12 *yojanas* long unless the author meant the city-state of Dwarka which embraced within its limits Kusasthali-Dwarka, Nageswar and the port of Aramda or Ārambhadvāra (the first entrance to Dwarka) also. At Warwala near Aramda, there is enough ground water even now. The orchard referred to in the epic could have existed here. The availability of ground water here was known to Krishna since he is said to have got water for Rukmini from a spring near Suvarnatīrtha. The expedition in 1998 brought to light several stone anchors and a berthing place for ships at Aramda, but the main Dwarka city at the mouth of Gomati had provided berthing facility for sea-sailing vessels by modifying a ridge into a wharf.

Fig. 53. Lifting lead ingots from a ship-wreck of 18th century on Tamil Nadu coast.

Somnath

Various theories have been advanced by scientists for the submergence of Dwarka in the 2nd millennium BC. Among the causes for submergence, earthquake and subsidence of the coastal strip are cited; but the excavation in Dwarka does not indicate disturbance due to tectonic activity. If a rise in sea level was the main cause, other ports such as Prabhas and Somnath, which were contemporary with ancient Dwarka, must have also been submerged. Keeping this point in view we started underwater exploration in a limited area of the sea-bed near Somnath and Prabhas. It was found that a rock-cut channel in the nearshore region of Somnath has been submerged. Near this channel, a spheroid mooring stone and a three-holed stone anchor similar to those found in Dwarka waters have been recorded. The ancient port near Prabhas has also been partly swallowed by the sea.

The Department of Culture and Tamil Development of the government of Tamil Nadu was generous enough to extend financial assistance for undertaking joint offshore exploration of Poompuhar in Tamil Nadu. It is a legendary city said to have been swallowed by the sea.

HISTORY FROM MYTHOLOGY – DISCOVERY OF LEGENDARY DWARKA

Mythology is based on a historical event or personality or both but embellished with miracles, folklores and poetic exaggerations. The Kurukshetra-Sonepat region has been a bone of contention and epoch-making battles were fought here in the Mahabharata and medieval periods. N.R. Ray thinks that there is,

> nothing antecedently improbable in the story of *Bhāratayuddha*. Even if the *Bhārathayuddha-Katha* was a myth, it is not a *mithya,* not fictional or illusory. It is a true story of a society of a particular period and

region. A myth is a complex cultural reality, the foremost function of which is to reveal the exemplary models of all significant human activities in a given society from birth to death. Indeed myths are the most proud and meaningful possessions of all early pre-Industrial Revolution societies. They provide the living entities by supplying models of human behaviour (Ray, N.R., in *Gupta and Ramachandran* (ed.) 1976, ix).

The historian is not only a collector of facts, but also a scientist in search of laws governing social growth. He has to study myths and symbols as much as he studies archaeological data. The common man who has no time or inclination to dwell upon spiritual insight and philosophic concepts is satisfied with mythology and simple rituals which have held the society together. Legends are woven around a unique religious or political leader or social reformer who has come to the rescue of the society in danger of extinction. Rama and Krishna are such leaders. The *Rāmāyana* and *Mahābhārata* are micro or macro history highlighting the dominant urges and moves as well as values of the society. Krishna is the dominant personality of *Mahābhārata* and was easily approachable even by the poorest. He went to the rescue of one and all in distress. He was not only a great social thinker and reformer but also practised what he preached. He would not tolerate cruelty and injustice. Kamsa had to be killed because he had put Vasudeva and Devaki in prison and killed children too. Again, it is Krishna who rescued the *gopis* from the clutches of Naraka and symbolically married them to restore their social status. He had to urge Arjuna to discharge his duty as a Kshatriya and fight the greedy Kaurava princes. The sole aim of Krishna was to reestablish *dharma* which was in danger. In short Krishna was an embodiment of intellectual and spiritual glory and at the same time a practical person. No other person has influenced the course of India's history, religion, philosophy, art and literature as Krishna has done.

The archaeologist and other scientists want verifiable evidence to accept Krishna as a historical person. He is said to have built Dwarka city to rehabilitate the Yadavas who migrated from Mathura under his leadership in the wider interest of the subjects of Mathura, which was threatened by Jarasandha's invasions. The question for the archaeologist was whether the city of Dwarka really existed and was submerged. If it did exist, can we find some traces of the city in the sea. It is this problem which set in motion the search for Dwarka. In 1936 Hirananda Sastry excavated parts of Bet Dwarka island which is traditionally known as Kusasthali where Krishna built Dwarka. H.D. Sankalia excavated in modern Dwarka on the bank of Gomati River and came to the conclusion that it was the Dwarka mentioned in *Skanda Purāna* and dated it to 1st century BC-AD, but this did not solve the problem as the Mahabharata War could not have been a post-Mauryan event, as there are references in *Kāṭhaka Samhitā* (X-6), *Kauśitaki Brāhmaṇa* (VII. 4) and *Śānkhyayana Śrauta Sutra* (III.4) to some of the personalities of *Mahābhārata. Panini* mentions Vasudeva, Arjuna, Bhima, Bhishma, Yudhishtira and Kunti. In *Chāndogya Upanishad* (III.17.6), Devakiputra is clearly mentioned. The Krishna cult had become so popular by the 2nd century BC that Heliodorus, the Greek ambassador in the court of Bhagadatta of Ujaini, in his inscription put up at Vidisa (Bedsa) calls himself *Parama Bhāgavata* who erected a pillar in honour of Vasudeva, *deva-deva*. The past which a historian studies is not a dead past but is a past, which is still living in the present. This is totally true of the *Mahābhārata*. The historian studies the thought that lies behind a past event. The facts do not come pure and are embroidered by myths and legends. It is for the historian to get to the core of the fact relieving it of poetic exaggerations and miracles. The vitality of Indian civilisation noticeable in the Indus civilisation five thousand years ago has enabled it to survive many calamities – natural and manmade – as well as the onslaughts by invaders. The Indus Valley people were peace-loving and tolerant. Indian culture could absorb essential elements of alien cultures as seen in Gandhara art. The historian has to get his facts right and interpret them in the light of the value system of the society, which is upheld throughout the age.

8

Poompuhar and Lakshadveep

The ancient port city of Poompuhar was not confined to the present mouth of the River Kaveri near Vanagiri. It extended northward up to Kilaiyur, where the ancient brick wharf was found, and further southward up to Chinnavanagiri, if not up to Tranquebar. Terracotta ringwells and large storage jars, datable to 1st-5th century AD, have been found in situ in the intertidal zones near Vanagiri and Tranquebar. Offshore survey opposite the present mouth of Kaveri and further seaward resulted in discovering brick structures in 5 to 7 m water depth. Only those parts of the structures exposed in low tide could be photographed but not underwater parts owing to poor visibility caused by continuous battering of waves in shallow waters.

There are disintegrated brick structures in the intertidal zone from Padupet to Vanagiri and remnants of brick and stone structures in 5 to 7 m depth, but they need to be surveyed intensively. The shipwreck in the site PMR 1 and the large oval-shaped structure in deeper waters at PMR 2 are proposed to be carefully excavated soon.

THIRTEENTH MARINE ARCHAEOLOGICAL EXPEDITION, 1992

The main objective of the expedition was to search for seaward extension of the submerged city of Poompuhar and determine its landward and seaward limits, if possible.

During the present expedition, the intertidal zone and offshore area between Nayakankuppam in the north and Vanagiri in the south were explored in water depths of 5 to 7 m. The shipwreck in PMR I was excavated and a stone structure at 23 m depth was identified.

In zone 2, geophysical surveys revealed three objects which were manually examined by the diver-archaeologists and confirmed as structures.

Structure No. 1. This structure was located at a water depth of 23 m which is about 5 km off the shore. It is semi-circular in shape. Its total peripheral length is 85 m and the distance between two arms is 13 m. The height of the object on the outer edge is 3 m, while on the inner side, the maximum height is 1 m. The height of the eastern arm is greater than that of the western arm, the width of the arms varying from 3 to 6 m. The centre of the object is covered with sediments, but hand-fanning showed that the central part is rocky at a depth of 10 to 15 cm. On the northern side of the object, an open space with a few rounded stones was found. Divers observed growth of thick marine organisms like oyster shells and gargorian on the structure, but in the section some courses of masonry are visible. Airlift operations in the southern side of the object showed a few rectangular and square blocks. Rock and sediment samples have been collected for analysis.

Structures No. 2 and 3 (about 40 m north of structure no. 1) Two structures were found lying in east-west direction. The distance between these objects is 10 m. The circumference of each object is not more than 15 m and the height is about 2 m. There are a number of wide cracks in the objects. A few dressed stone blocks, 2 m in length, 1.5 m in breadth and 1 m in height, are lying near the smaller objects which measure 100 x 60 x 20 cm.

In zone 3, one shipwreck was located during the last expedition and the same was relocated in this season with the help of the echosounder and side scan sonar at a water depth of 19 m. Diver-archaeologists used the metal detectors to trace the buried extension of the shipwreck. The search confirmed that about 75 per cent of the ship is buried in the sediment. The total length of the wreck which lies northeast-southwest, is about 100 m, its breadth being 25-30 m and height about 3 m, perhaps more. It is a wooden hulled ship, the bottom of which is plated with copper sheets. Two round holes were noticed in the ship deck. Airlift operation inside the hole revealed a few stone blocks that had fallen from the deck.

A number of lead ingots were found in the wreck (Fig. 53). Among them, four types were noticed. Type 1: Long oval-shaped ingot: inscription W and date 1792 on one surface and the symbol of VOC on the other. Type 2: Oval-shaped ingot flat with the inscription mentioned in Type 1 above. Type 3: Long oval-shaped ingot punched with a crown symbol below which the alphabet 'D'occurs. Type 4: Rectangular ingot without any inscription or symbol on the obverse while the reverse has the VOC symbol.

During the previous expedition and the one under discussion, ring wells were noticed in the intertidal zone of the excavated areas near Chinnavanagiri, where the habitational site is also preserved. On the basis of associated pottery, the ringwell can be dated to 2nd century BC. On one of the potsherds the Brahmi sign for 'Ma' is also inscribed. On palaeographic grounds, it is assignable to 2nd century BC.

In the Bay of Bengal, the high energy zone extends up to a depth of 8-9 m, as it is very much disturbed by high waves, currents and tides. It is very difficult to presume that some structures, particularly of bricks, which were mostly used in Sangam period, would have survived intact in the high energy zone. It is only the stone structures which are likely to provide a clue to understand the plans of the buildings.

As far as deep water structures in zone 2 are concerned, there are several views about the purpose they might have served. The local fishermen consider the big oval-shaped structure as a temple. T.C.S. Rao also agrees with this view. According to him, the bigger object which is hollow at the centre is the main temple with a *garbhagriha* and the two smaller objects, which are situated north of the bigger objects, may be the front pillars of the temple. The outer edges of both the objects are in the same alignment. Although apsidal rock-cut temples of Mahendravarma period are known at Mahabalipuram, it is too early to say that an apsidal temple of stone existed here.

Exploration in Lakshadveep. The first expedition to Byramgore reefs in Lakshadveep island group was a joint endeavour with the help of the Indian Navy. The East India Company wreck Byramgore could not be located precisely. In the next expedition, the MAC discovered two steel-hulled shipwrecks of 19th century. One of them was documented (Fig. 54).

SEA LEVEL FLUCTUATION

It would be relevant here to compare the sea level change recorded by Larsen in his survey of coastal settlements of Bahrain where ancient Kassite ports are swallowed by the sea. He says that a fall in the sea level was followed by a period of submergence between 3000 and 5000 BC. Similar

Fig. 54. Wreckage of a steel-hulled ship of 19th century in Lakshadveep water.

regressions and transgressions of the sea can be postulated for the Gulf of Kutch and the Arabian Sea. When the sea level was lower before 2000 BC, Kusasthali seems to have been built and a century or later it was partly damaged and then Krishna built the first Dwarka and still later the mainland Dwarka. Both were submerged in the 16th century BC.

The rise in the sea level attributed by Tewari and Negi to planetary conjuctions (See Tewari and Negi, 1988 and Negi, 1999) seems to be convincing. Subsequent to the destruction of both Dwarkas three temples built successively on the mainland at Dwarka were also destroyed by the sea (Rao, 1999). Thus, the existence and submergence of Dwarka or Dvaravati mentioned in the *Māhabhārata* cannot be disputed in the light of overwhelming archaeological evidence. There may be some controversy regarding the date of Dwarka city. The date 18th-17th century BC is assigned to Dwarka on the basis of TL-date as well as palaeographical evidence besides the well-known date of Late Harappan pottery, seal and inscription found in Bet Dwarka (see Rao, S.R., 2001).

A SERIOUS ACCIDENT

On 16 May 1994, I went to Dabolim airport in Goa to board a plane for Bangalore. As my ticket was not confirmed I waited until the plane left and came back disappointed to Panaji to take a private bus to Bangalore. Before narrating how the accident took place, I would like to refer to the Ganesa temple built under my direction at Goa. About two hundred families of scientists and other staff in NIO were celebrating Ganesh Chaturthi festival every year but they needed a temple. I took the initiative and with their co-operation it was possible to build the temple in NIO colony in 1992 (for details see *Ganesh Pratisthan, Souvenir* 1992.)

On 16 May 1994, the luxury bus of Janata Travels arrived at Panaji late in the evening and I was given a seat behind the driver. There were two Muslim drivers for driving alternately. After the bus went a few miles the second driver asked a young passenger to pay the bus fare. The young man said he had already paid the fare to the bus agent at Panaji. An hour later the driver again demanded the fare from the passenger who had already paid it. A heated argument ensued. I told the driver that if the boy has not paid the fare at Goa he would pay it in Bangalore as he did not have enough money with him to pay twice. The rude driver forced the young man to get down at Ponda. A few minutes after the bus left Ponda bus station, it hit a scooter. There was no injury to the rider but the residents of Ponda surrounded the bus, demanded Rs. 500 as cost of repairing the scooter. After much argument the driver paid the amount but the two drivers started quarrelling among themselves and hurled abuses at each other. The passengers were fed up with the behaviour of the drivers. When the bus reached Hubli at midnight, the second driver, who had demanded double fare from the passenger, was however pursuaded by the first driver to drive the rest of the distance to which he agreed. I was awake throughout the night. At about 6 a.m. on the 17th, about 5 km before reaching the district town Chitradurga, the bus driver tried to overtake a scooter but failed to avoid a lorry speeding from the opposite direction. There was a head-on-collision which resulted in the death of four persons including both the drivers of the lorry and bus. In the collision I was hit by the driver's seat. My hip joint was dislodged and both the bones of the my right leg were fractured. Heavy bleeding started from my leg, forehead and the nose-bridge. I lost consciousness for about 30 minutes and later all that I remember is that I was lying on the footpath. A stranger took me to Chitradurga hospital in his van and admitted me there. I gave him my visiting card and asked him to telephone my wife Kamala and daughter-in-law Meena at Bangalore which he promptly did and came back to ask me if he could be of any further assistance. I looked at him to express my deep debt of gratitude. This timely help saved my life. It was perhaps God's wish that I should live for some more time to publish the Dwarka report and take up another mission of building a temple in Bangalore. My attempt at Bangalore to trace the stranger who saved my life bore no fruit. The doctor in-charge of the hospital in Chitradurga attended to my injuries and gave necessary first aid, but the bleeding from my nose did not stop. I was extremely thirsty. Two doctors and one senior nurse were attending to other injured persons. Incessant bleeding and severe pain forced me to cry for help. A teenage nurse standing by my side could not do anything except offer some coconut water. Out of despair, I pushed down the wash basin. The noise attracted the doctor. When I explained to him my agony, he asked me to buy some medicine, but I had no money. I had lost all things except a leather bag in which I had kept the entire 300 page manuscript of my report on Dwarka excavation with 100 photographs.

As soon as my son Gopal at Hospet got the message from Bangalore, he contacted the doctor in the hospital, ascertained my condition and left Hospet town in a car for Chitradurga. On arrival he saw me lying with blood-smeared face. After some further medical aid was given to me, he took me to Bangalore in an ambulance. On the way I was chanting Sanskrit verses (*slokas*) and devotional songs on Sri Krishna which my mother had taught. I reached St. John Hospital at 8 p.m. where Meena and Kamala were anxiously waiting for my arrival. In the Emergency Ward, I was examined by Dr. Narayan who was told by the senior surgeon that CT scanning was necessary to make sure that there is no brain injury, before I could be administered anesthesia for operation. He was suspecting a small blocking of the blood vessel, but finally the scanning did not show any serious blocking. The orthopaedic surgeon then set the displaced hip-joint immediately as more than 12 hours had passed after the dislocation had taken place. The bones in the leg were fractured and overlapping. I was under local anesthesia when a hole was being drilled across the femur to insert a steel rod from which weights were suspended to bring the bones to their original position in due course. With right leg plastered, I was in bed for 35 days. Sundaresh and Puttappa Lambani from NIO and Vasu from Keladi attended on me for several days. Kamala, Meena and Gopal were constantly attending to all my needs. My grandson Upendra and grand-daughter Nandini did their best. Relatives and friends came to see me on the 18th. His Holiness Sri Satya Pramoda Tirtha Swamiji of Uttaradi Math sent *prasada* with his blessings. Mr. Veerendra Hegde from Dharmasthala came to see me and gave the *prasada* of Sri

Manjunatheswara. I was often sleepless at night due to severe pain. This made me wake up Vasu and Lambani very often. On 22nd June the orthopaedic surgeon found considerable improvement in my condition and permitted me to go home with plastered leg. I could use a wheel chair and walk slowly with crutches, with Meena's and Kamala's help. One night, after I had a stroke and my speech was affected, I was immediately admitted in Sekhar Hospital, where Dr. Jayaprakash told me later that I was stable. A couple of days later, I was taken to St. John's Hospital for further investigation. It took three months for me to recover fully and resume my normal work. Although I could not take to the sea, I continued to write my report on Marine Archaeological Expeditions for publishing my book, *The Lost City of Dwarka*. Mr. Pradeep Kumar Goel of Aditya Prakashan published it in 1999. Thus happily ended my adventure in search of the legendary Dwarka.

9

Miscellany

FELLOWSHIPS AND AWARDS

Jawaharlal Nehru Fellowship

The Jawaharlal Nehru Fellowship is a very prestigeous award given every year to enable a scholar to undertake or continue research. I was selected for the award in 1977 by a Committee headed by Dr. Karan Singh, the scholar prince of Jammu and Kashmir. This enabled me to continue my research on decipherment of the Indus script in India and abroad. It involved a careful study of Vedic and classical Sanskrit, Indo-Iranian and ancient Greek languages and Semitic scripts. My knowledge of Dravidian languages helped me to assess the attempts made by scholars who considered Indus language to be Dravidian. I published my article in *Indian and Foreign Review* (IFR) in 1978. A letter from F.N. Souza published in IFR reads, "I want to congratulate Dr. Rao heartily; I'd say his findings deserve a Nobel," which made several scholars view my decipherment with the seriousness it deserved, but some of others refused to see the truth.

My retirement from ASI in 1980 was a great blessing in disguise, as it gave me an opportunity to work for the discovery of the legendery Dwarka city submerged in the sea.

FIE Foundation Award

This award established in Maharashtra by Fuel Injection Engineers to promote individual achievements in the field of Industrial and Technical progress and also in Humanities was given to me in 1991 by the then Prime Minister of India, S. Chandrasekhar for "Outstanding achievement (at the senior level) discovery of Dwarka". It carried a citation and cash award of Rs. 25,000. Among other scientists and humanists who were given the award were Dr. Nayyar, Managing Director of Hindustan Aeronautics Ltd.

Gupta Foundation Award

The industrialist and philantropist of Eluru, a small town in Andhra Pradesh, Mr. Mohan Gupta has established a Trust known as Gupta Foundation to promote science, art and culture. The selection committee of the Foundation selected me for receiving this award in 1994 for achievement in the field of Marine Archaeology resulting in the discovery of the legendary city of Dwarka. The earlier recipients of this award are M.S. Subba Lakshmi, famous musician and Dr. Padma Subramanyam, dancer. Eluru town wore for the occasion a festive look. *Shahnai* was played in the evening which was pleasing to the ears. Young, beautifully dressed damsels in traditional Andhra sarees welcomed the guests. Among the celebrities attending the award function were Dr. Arudra, a renowned Telugu writer. In the decorated *pandal* where the function was arranged, there hung in the background a large painting on cloth depicting the legendary city of submerged Dwarka. The Gupta

Foundation has specialised itself in the art of sandalwood carving. It also exports sandalwood chips to Japan and other countries where it is used for incense-burning in temples. Here is an example of industrialists promoting art and culture.

KARNATAKA RAJYA PRASASTI

This award of the government of Karnataka is given to those who have made outstanding contribution to the development of the state in various fields. I was given a gold medal and a memento by the Chief Minister, Sri Ramakrishna Hegde, in 1985 in recognition of the preservation of the cultural heritage by way of conservation of Chalukyan, Hoysala and Vijayanagar temples in the state and improving the environment of the monuments at Pattadakal, Aihole and Badami. The Pattadakal group of temples is declared a 'World Heritage' by UNESCO.

WORLD SHIP TRUST AWARD 1991

This award was instituted by the World Ship Trust, UK for the first time for individual excellence in Marine Archaeology. The slogan of the Trust is 'Never Again' which is in memory of the ship which sank with a large crew in the course of underwater exploration. I was selected for the first award for my exploration and excavation of submerged Dwarka. The award was given by His Excellency, the Governor of Karnataka in 1992 (Fig. 55).

Conservation of Unprotected Temples by Sri Dharmasthala Manjunatheswara Dharmotthana Trust: Dr. Veerandra Hedge of Dharmasthala, a philantropist as well as educationist, is the pontiff of the Siva temple of Manjunatheswara at Dharmasthala in Dakshina Kannada district of Karnataka. Although the temple is dedicated to Siva, the priests are Vaishnavites (devotees of Vishnu). It is managed by Hegde, a Jain devotee. The large income from the offerings in cash

Fig. 55. World Ship Trust Award.

and kind made by the devotees is partly used for the upliftment of the poor and promotion of art and culture. Another activity of the Trust is conservation of ancient unprotected temples of archaeological, historical and artistic importance in Karnataka. As honorary advisor to SDMD Trust, of which Mr. Hegde is the president, I visited as many as forty temples between 1992 and 1999 and drew up an inspection note to enable the archaeological engineers employed by the Trust to carry out the repairs to temples. I inspected the conservation works in progress and gave suitable instructions to the engineers. Since 1993 the Trust has conserved as many as 32 ancient temples ranging in date from 8th century to 18th century AD belonging to Chola, Chalukyan, Hoysala, Vijayanagar, Nayaka and Wodeyar periods (sec. APP III). The temple at Tagadur in Mandya district is an example of conservation of a badly damaged monument (Figs. 56-57).

The project has created a new awareness of the cultural heritage of India and the need for its preservation. Initially we were doubtful whether the villagers would contribute their share of the cost of repairs, but soon we found that they were anxious to do so. I am glad that after retirement from ASI I could participate in the preservation of our neglected heritage. The conservation work involved immense touring, inspection, and attention to structural problems, but the reward is the pleasure of giving a new lease of life to beautiful temples.

KARNATAKA CHITRAKALA PARISHATH, BANGALORE

As a trustee of the Fine Arts Academy of Karnataka, which has an excellent collection of leather puppets, paintings and other art objects, I had an occasion to regulate the working of the Academy and tried to give an independent status to the College of Fine Arts run by the Trust. The college is affiliated to the Bangalore University. Chitrakala Parishath made great progress under the patronage of Sri Devaraj Urs, the then chief minister of Karnataka. He gave the prime land for the construction of a building for the Academy next to government guest house on Kumara Krupa Road. Mr. T.P. Issar, secretary to the govt., the famous artist Dr. Roerich and I were associated with the selection and approval of a design for the building to a large extent and also supervised its construction. It now houses the Kejriwal collection of Roerich's paintings besides the Academy's

Fig. 56. Lakshmī Nārāyaṇa temple in ruin before conservation, Tagadur.

Fig. 57. Lakshmī Nārāyaṇa temple after conservation by SDMD Trust.

paintings and other antiquities as well. One of the important contributions of the Academy is the publication of *Traditional Paintings of Karnataka*, authored by me and B.V.K. Sastry. It is hoped that the reconstituted Trust Board will bring out more such art books. The academy conducts classes in fine arts as a course work of the students, and also lends its halls for holding exhibitions. Before his demise, Dr. S. Roerich wrote a letter to me appointing me as one of the trustees of Satyadhama, an estate where Roerich's paintings and other art objects of his family are to be housed, but the government is yet to implement it.

RESTRUCTURING ARCHAEOLOGICAL SURVEY

The ASI is the largest organisation in the world looking after Indian monuments, archaeological and epigraphical research, conducting excavations, and supporting the universities financially and technically in carrying out excavations. In fact, ASI is the foremost leader which lays down the policy in all archaeological matters in the country. Over the years its leadership has suffered and problems have multiplied.

During the last ten years, the Archaeological Survey had no professional archaeologist as director-general. The bureaucrats from the Indian Administrative Service (IAS) who could not understand the problems, or even if they understood, they could not find solutions due to red tapism to which they were accustomed, became a stumbling block in the progress of archaeological research and maintanence of monuments which constitute the richest cultural heritage of India. The post of Joint Director General was also held by officers of the Indian Administrative Service with the result that the professional archaeologists at director's level had no choice of going up and guiding the destinies of the survey.

In May 2000 the new minister for culture (including archaeology) in the Central Government, Sri Ananth Kumar, who took interest in ASI, appointed a Committee for recommending suitable measures to make ASI result-oriented and to reorganise the Institute of Archaeology. I was invited to be a member of the review committee. The committee recommended modifying rules of recruitment to the post of the director-general so that the post could be held by a professional archaeologist. Among other recommendations, the expeditious publication of excavation reports and preservation of sites need special mention. It also emphasised that Class I posts of ASI should be filled through All India Examination specifying the subjects in which they should specialise.

MEN AND MATTERS

Sir Mortimer Wheeler (Fig. 59)

Robert Eric Mortimer Wheeler was born in 1890 in Glasgow. His father, Mortimer Wheeler, worked for *Blackie's Encyclopaedia.* His mother was well educated. R.E.M. Wheeler took a degree in classics from the University of London and later the Master's degree also. He served as a captain in the Royal Artillery in the First World War. As an archaeologist, Wheeler appreciated Pitt-Rivers' technique of archaeological excavation based on stratigraphy. His excavation at the fort of Segontium received much publicity. His great ambition was to establish an institute for training young archaeologists, and to achieve it he accepted the directorship of the London Museum and got established a post-graduate diploma course in field-archaeology in the University of London. His excavation at Verulanium and Maiden Castle brought him great reputation as an archaeologist. He put in a lot of effort to rouse the interest of the public in archaeology. Wheeler's idea of establishing an institute of archaeology in London materialised in 1937.

During World War II, he served in the army in North Africa. In 1944 he joined the Archaeological Survey of India (ASI) as director-general and with the discipline and drive of a professional soldier he reorganised the ASI and started the Taxila School of Field Archaeology to train young Indian scholars in scientific digging, three-dimensional recording, photography, surveying, drawing, analysis and interpretation of data and publication of excavation report.

But Wheeler, in his anxiety to connect Harappa with Hariyupia of *Rigveda,* not only interpreted the peripheral wall of the city as a defense against the invading Aryans but also tried to identify the culture of Cemetery H as that of the Aryans. He interpreted the earlier culture of cemetery R37 as that of the non-Aryan inhabitants of Harappa. He wrote "on circumstantial evidence Indra stands accused" of destroying Harappa. This remark, while pleasing the archaeologists and historians who had believed in Marshall's interpretation of Indus civilisation being non-Aryan, raised a controversy which is still troubling historians. Subsequent excavation at Harappa by Prof. G.F. Dales has established that there is continuity in the cultural assemblage of Cemetery R37 and Cemetery H. Further, anthropologist, Kennedy has concluded that there is no ethnic variation between the Cemetery R37 and CemeteryH population as can be made out from the human skeletal remains. These observations put an end to Wheeler's speculation about Aryan invasion of Harappa and Mohenjodaro.

It must, however, be said to the credit of Wheeler that as a professional archaeologist, he changed his opinion and accepted new evidence. He wrote (Wheeler, 1968, p. 47),

> For the present it would be premature to conjecture that the Lower City was fortified in military sense though it is increasingly clear that massive flood-defenses were undertaken.

I think that he came to this conclusion after seeing the anti-flood peripheral walls and podiums on which houses stood at Lothal as in the case of Harappa also.

I had an opportunity to undergo training in scientific excavation in the School of Field Archaeology at Sisupalgarh in March 1948, when Wheeler was still in charge of ASI. He visited the trench in which I was working and asked me whether I knew drawing section of excavated strata. I told him that I am yet to learn it. He immediately went to the camp and sent the Senior Draftsman Raghubir Singh to help me in drawing plans and sections in an intelligible way. From this single instance, I could understand that he was very keen on training young archaeologists in all branches of the subject.

Long after his retirement from ASI in 1948, Wheeler as secretary of the British Academy visited my excavation at Lothal in 1959 and was pleased to see that I was training young scholars in the School of Archaeology at Lothal. He remarked, "I am glad that the third generation is undergoing training in field archaeology." Our camp looked like a military camp, everything done according to schedule. The students had to learn drawing, survey, photography and digging following Wheelerian technique. Field notes were maintained with meticulous care.

After going round the excavated trenches, I asked him whether he could see any defense in the military sense at Lothal. He said, "No."

An important quality of Wheeler was to be firm in his opinion about the assessment of other's work. After visiting the dock at Lothal he emphatically said and wrote, "It was a dock (without doubt)." He spared some time in the British Academy to discuss with me some of my findings at Lothal and later agreed to write a foreword to my book, *Lothal and the Indus Civilisation* (1973). An important advise given by him was that we should not be very emphatic in our conclusions since new evidence may necessitate changing our opinion. Wheeler's contribution to archaeology in India lies in giving a new generation of well-trained archaeologists, who could take good care of ancient monuments and promote archaeological research in India. The succeeding generations have not failed him. Wheeler had an ambition to establish an Institute of Archaeology in London University, which he achieved. I too had a small ambition to establish an Alphabet Gallery to demonstrate the decipherment of Indus script. Twenty-three years after my retirement from service, my dream came true with the establishment of the Alphabet Gallery, *Akṣraram (Lipi Veethika)* in Rashtriya Sanskrit Vidyapeetha (Deemed University) at Tirupati, in Andhra Pradesh in 2004. Besides exhibiting replicas of some Indus seals, the methodology of decoding Indus script is also explained through charts put up in the galleries. A catalogue of exhibits is also published. I am greatly indebted to Dr. V.R. Panchamukhi, Chancellor and Prof. D. Prahladachar, Vice-Chancellor, for their whole-hearted cooperation in providing funds, building and staff. Panchamukhi is a reputed economist and Sanskritist. Prahladachar is a well-known scholar in Sanskrit and Veda and both are able administrators too. Their love for research induced them to spare no efforts to give a shape to the Alphabet Gallery.

AJNEYA (SACHCHIDANANDA VATSYAYAN)

Some time in the month of May 1984, I received a telephone call from Sacchidananda Vatsyayan whom, I vaguely remembered, I had met in the company of Rai Kishan Das in Benaras. Vatsyayan (pen-name Ajneya) took me by surprise by inviting me to deliver a talk on my decipherment of Indus script which had received enough comments, both adverse and appreciative, from scholars of various shades.

To receive an invitation from such a renowned scholar, eminent poet, lover of art and critic as Sacchidananda was an honour. I readily agreed to attend the Third Annual Seminar (*Vyākhyānamālā*) on Indian culture, literature and art to be held in memory of another great personality of India, namely, Rai Kishan Das who devoted his entire life to the promotion of Indian art and culture on the lines of what Anaṇḍa Coomaraswamy had done for promoting Indian art in the western world.

Sacchidananda Vatsyayan (born in 1911) hailed from a family of renowned scholars. His father, Dr. Hirananda Sastry, was an epigraphist and Sanskrit scholar. Ajneya had by 1985 attained a very high position among the internationally known writers. I had read his two books, *Island In the Stream* (1980) and *Truculent Clay* (1982), the former being an English translation of his Hindi original *Bhavanti* and the latter of *Nadi Ke Dvipa*. Although I had learnt Hindi language in high school and subsequently acquired knowledge of spoken Hindi, I enjoyed reading Vatsyayan's English versions. Vatsyayan is an academic, an army officer and editor of *Writer's Journal*. Vatsayayan's Hindi poems are translated into English, Russian, German, Serbo-Croatian, Italian, Danish and Swedish languages. He has published eight collections of short stories and more than a dozen volumes each of poetry and essays. His travelogues are very popular as are the novels which have seen many editions. His experiment with theme and craft in *Nadi Ke Dvipa* had been denounced by some but acclaimed by many. The author's rendering of the Hindi novel into English is a masterpiece among novels.

When I met him at Lucknow I felt here is a unique personality speaking rarely and that too very few words. In the seminar he spoke in chaste Hindi. For a while I felt diffident to converse with him in Hindi, but soon he made me relax by speaking in English. I gained some courage and spoke in Hindi in private conversation. He told me that he was surprised to find me speak in Hindi with proper intonations. Ananda Krishna, son of late Rai Kishan Das, started asking me about my decipherment. Ajneya who had gone through my paper remarked, "I am glad you have made a bold and new approach." I felt encouraged. I got a few doubts of mine regarding various shades of meaning each word in Vedic Sanskrit had. His explanation was very convincing. I was trying to "imbibe the invisible atmosphere of the genius". What surprised me is that in spite of some setbacks in his private life, he rose to Himalayan heights as a literary genius and a great promoter of Indian art and culture.

In spite of his illness, Ajneya never gave up editing and writing. His life is a monumental example of courage, devotion to one's work and a commitment to promote Indian art, culture and literature. As editor of *Writer's Journal*, he set new trends in the literary field. Ajneya's *Bhavanti* (1971) and *Sasvati* (1979) present an integrated vision of the writer's struggle with his medium. Perhaps he was reflecting from his personal life. "In his *Undated journal* he tries to present experience in all its variety and spontaneity."

In 1984, Ajneya was taken ill and was being looked after by a devout disciple; yet he never gave an impression that his health was failing . His courage and convictions served me as a guide for further research in the field of Marine Archaeology at Dwarka and decipherment of Indus script.

Appendix

PROBLEMS OF DECODING INDUS SCRIPT

(Fig. 10 to 17 in the text)

The architects of the Indus civilisation were literate. The excavations at Harappa, Mohenjodaro, Lothal, Kalibangan, Dholavira, Surkotada and other sites in the Indian sub-continent have yielded more than 3,000 seals and sealings inscribed in a mixed writing of pictures and cursive signs. There is no clue in the form of long sentences or repetitive phrases, as in the case of Brahmi writing of the 3rd century BC, from which one could deduce the language and purpose of seals. The Egyptian hieroglyphic writing could be deciphered because of the 'Rosetta Stone' in which a known script and a known language appear along with the unknown script. In the case of Indus script, no bilingual or biscriptal writing is available in any of the 3200 seals and sealings.

The Indus script presents another difficulty in decoding it owing to the presence of cursive (linear) signs, side by side pictorials of man, pipal leaf, bird, scorpion, hill, field and insects (Fig. 1). Hence, the decipherer is at a loss to know whether all the pictoral as well as non-pictoral signs, should be read as ideogrprahs in which ideas or actions are indicated or as logographs which stand for words or as signs, having a sound value only. This can be decided only when the total number of basic signs as distinct from compound signs, is known.

Direction of Writing

The writing on Indus seals was from right to left and the mirror impressions of the seal inscription should be read from right to left (from head to tail of the animal).

Evolution of Indus Script (Fig. 12)

The recent excavations at Lothal (1955-62), Rojdi, Dholavira (1987-95) and Kalibangan in India and the renewed excavations by G.F. Dales at Mohenjodaro (1965) and Harappa (1987-88) provide the much needed chronological basis for tracing the evolution of writing from a partly pictorial script into a pure cursive (linear) script omitting all the pictorials of the early levels such as the pipal leaf, hill, field, scorpion, plants and animals. In the early levels, both cursive and pictorial signs occurred together. Further structural analysis of the purely cursive signs of the late levels went a long way in determining the number of basic signs (Fig. 12).

BASIC SIGNS

The first breakthrough in the decipherment of Indus script was achieved with the identification of basic signs.

The number of basic signs in the early Harappan script of 2500-2000 BC is 62 including 24 pictures while in the late-Harappan script of 2000-1600 BC, the number of basic signs gets reduced to 24 (Fig. 13A-B) since pictorials and some of the alternate basic signs are omitted. With such a small number of basic signs, the Indus script could only be phonetic wherein each sign had a sound value, which may be a single sound as in the alphabetic system or a syllabic one. The identification of basic signs was possible because of the recognition of two distinguishing features of the Indus script, namely, (1) attaching short slashes (strokes) for indicating vowel value of consonantal signs, and (2) joining two or more basic signs to form conjunct consonants (*samyukta akṣaras*) or syllables, e.g., *Rka, pta* or *ark, pat,* etc. These two features are noticeable in Brāhmī script of 3rd century BC. The purpose of attaching strokes was to indicate vowel value of consonantal signs and ligaturing was a technique invented for forming conjunct consonants (*samyukta akṣaras*) by joining signs. The Asokan inscriptions are good examples for continuance of these two techniques of Harappan script by later Brahmi scribes but there is one minor difference and that is the medial vowel value of the consonantal sign in Brāhmī script depended on the direction and number of strokes (*mātras),* while in Harappan and late Harappan scripts, it is mainly the number of slashes that determine the medial vowel value.

The Harappan script had separate signs for initial vowels *a, ā, ae*(*u*) and *ɩ ɔ*(*o*). Brahmi also had initial vowels *a, ā ae*(*u*) and *ao* (*o*). Brāhmī also had initial vowels *a, ā, i, e, o,* It is fairly clear that the Brāhmī script is evolved from the late-Harappan cursive script (Fig. 15).

Phonetic Value of basic Cursive Signs

Having identified the basic Indus signs as elemental forms devoid of additional strokes, the phonetic value of each sign had to be ascertained. To avoid a subjective element by presuming the language to be Aryan or Dravidian, the principle of proceeding from the known to the unknown was adopted and this was possible by comparing Indus script with the known alphabetic script of the semites (Hebrew, Phoenician and early Canaanite). Their phonetic script of 23 consonantal signs was in use in the 15th-11th century BC (Driver, G.R., 1976, 104-106). *The comparison of Indus signs with semitic signs showed that 17 signs in the two scripts are identical (Fig. 14). It was therefore reasonable to assign the phonetic value of semitic signs to analogous basic cursive signs of the Late Indus script* which is found to have survived even in the mid-second millennium BC at Daimabad, Rangpur and Bet Dwarka. While reading 102 Indus inscriptions on the basis of the semitic phonetic value, the vocalic indicators attached to cursive signs of the former in the Harappan script had to be taken note of. The language indicated by the reading yielded words similar to those in ancient Sanskrit (old Indo-Aryan). For instance, the words *aeka* = one, *daś* = ten, *śata* = hundred, *śada* = eminent, *maha* = great, *pat-pat (pati)* = governor, master, *para* = supreme, *nana* = mother, *bhaga* = gracious Lord, patron, *vap* = create, *bhā* = brilliant, *pav(a)* = pure, *sah* = victorious, *pada* = foot, *śāsa* = ruler, and *pa* = protect. There are also words analogous to Avestan words, e.g., *hapta* = seven, *sah* = praise, *papa* = protecting, *gavva (gavaya), gah* = prayer, *atha* = fire, *baga* = bountiful, Lord, God, *ama* = power, etc. (Figs. 16a-b). One may wonder how an Old Indo-Aryan or Indo-Iranian language could be arrived at from the inscriptions in which the signs are given semitic phonetic value. The reason is that whereas the semitic script is purely consonantal, the Indus writing had vowel signs and conjunct consonants which enabled the Indus scribes to write an Indo-Aryan (Old Indo-Aryan) – Old Iranian language. As the Indus script was written in the Old Indo-Aryan language, the phonetic value of 'man' and 'fish' signs was derived on acrophonic principle from the Old

Indo-Aryan words namely, *nr/nara* for 'man' and *ś* from *śaphara* for a variety of 'fish'. The reading of inscriptions in which 'man' and 'fish' signs occur yields meaningful phonemes when the phonetic value *r* and *ś* is given to 'man' and 'fish' signs, respectively (Fig. 14). A few examples of phonemes in Old Indo-Aryan and Old Iranian words occuring in Indus inscriptions are given below.

Old Indo-Aryan Words (See Rao, S.R. 1991 and 2004)

ar = revere, get; *rka* (*arka*) = fire, sun; *arha* = able, deserving; *rta* = order; *tatrha* = of defender or saviour; *badra* (*bhadra*) = auspicious ; *dr* = split; *tr* = save; *pr* = protect; *sr* = flow; *śās* = ruler, commander; *śama* = peaceful; *saha* = victorious, *śah* = king; *śakka/śaka* = powerful; *śada* = eminent; *daśaha/daśaka* = tenth; *śamaha* = peace-maker; *aśa* = space, heaven, divine order in creation, etc. These readings further corroborate that the Indus language is closest semantically and morphologically to Old Indo-Aryan (OIA) and to some extent with Old Iranian. The speakers of these languages were fire-worshippers as attested by linguistic as well as archaeological evidence.

NUMERALS

The next stage of decipherment relates to long vertical lines numbering 1 to 10, 12 and 24 which correspond to the cardinals. The words for one, seven, ten and hundred in the Indus inscription are *aeka, hapta, daśa* and *śata* respectively. As such it would be reasonable to infer that the words for other cardinal numbers should be in OIA or OIR. Sometimes the numeral signs were used as phonograms, for example, the numeral sign for 111 (three) could designate either the number 3 or serve as suffix *tr* as in *pātr* or as root-noun as in *tra/trā* (save), or *tri* as in *tridha* = 'triply'. Arka (Fire God) is said to be of three forms (*tridha*), namely, fire, sun and lightening.

PICTURALS

There are in all 28 picturals in the early Indus inscriptions, but only 7 occur several times, and others occasionally, not more than 5 or 6 times in the entire lot of 3,200 seals and sealings. The picturals occuring more than 10 times are those depicting the bird, scorpion, pipal leaf *(ficus religiousa)* field, insect, hand, hill and bee. They are treated as phonograms and are given the value of the initial syllable of the words for these objects in Old Indo-Aryan. Hence, syllabic values *aśśv (aśvatha), has (hasta), kṣ/kṣatra, śak, vṛś, makṣ and adr* are given for pictures of pipal leaf, hand, field, bird, scorpion, bee and hill for which OIA words are *aśvatth, hasta, kṣatra, śakuna, vrścika, makṣa* and *adri*, respectively. They make meaningful phonemes in inscriptions.

In the early stage of Indus writing a picture which had a word value acquired a syllabic value which could be used in writing any word which consisted of that syllabic, or of which that syllabic was a component element. A couple of examples are given below:

1. The picture of scorpion stood for *vriscika* (OIA) which was used as syllabic *vrs'* and two other phonetic cursive signs for *h* and *a* were attached to it to write the compound word *vrs' + h+a = vrsha*, meaning manly and bountiful. It was also used to write *vrṣha + n = vrshan* or bountiful.
2. Similarly, the cross sign conveying the meaning cross or save (*tar* in sanskrit) was used as a determinative for saviour, or God followed by a word separator. It could also be used with scorpion sign (*vrsha*) and a sign for *n* to write *vrsha-n-tar.*
3. Pipal leaf sign for *asvattha* used syllabically *asv* or to write the names of persons *aśvaha* they, could write *aśvaha* and *aśvaka, aśva* which meant horse as well as fire in OIA (*Rigveda*).

4. The most common sign for man with the syllabic value r (derived from *nr/nara*) was used along with other cursive signs to write *r+ka = rka, arka* (fire) or meaning sun; similarly, it was used to write *r + ha = rha (arha)* meaning able.

Intially, the Indus language was largely more syllabic (see fig. 12 & 59) with hardly any prefixes or suffix added to the root-nouns, e.g., *rh, arh* (able or deserve) and *arha* (able person). Thus, symbols representing objects or words came to denote sounds as syllable. But most Indus inscriptions of early phase were not purely pictograph or indeographs. They were mainly syllabic evolved from pictographs a writing which was not yet alphabet, i.e. after acquiring phonetic value. The phonetic cursive signs with diacritics added to them for medial vocalic value. The technique of writing compound consonant must have enabled the Indus scribes to write Indo-European (Indo-Aryan and Iranian) languages which need vowel signs for easy and correct pronunciation (Fig. 59).

The simplification or codification of the intonations of Vedic vowel system by classical writers like Panini and still earlier by Yaska appears to have been done in the light of the prevailing writing of the alphabetic system as indicated by the Lothal inscriptions *a-p-a = apa, a-pa = apa, p-a-ka = paka; pa-rā-t-tṛ-ka-parāttraka*, etc. (Fig. 59). The late Indus script of Bet Dwarka inscription (Fig. 38) was writen from left to write. It reads *ma-hā-hā gacha-sha-ha-pā = mahhāgacha (mahākaccha = sea), shah (king)-pa* (protect = protector) conveying the sense 'sea lord, protect'. By 1500 BC the phoenicians were using the Indus signs for their consonantal value.

The possibility of the inscriptions of early Indus phase being hieratic which involved the use of a few determinatives and ideograms cannot be ruled out, but it must be remembered that in 2950 out of 3000 Indus inscriptions, there is always a cursive sign or a phonetised picture which had phonetic value. The majority of seals used for commercial purpose had a religious context such as offering prayer to God seeking his protection or to obtain gifts. The names of sacrifices – *Ekāha Aśṭaka, Aśvasatra* – and names of holy men – Kaśappa, Śara, Śasa, Sasa *Atri, Baka, Manu*, etc., are also mentioned in seals. Some names of regions or rivers such as *Bhadrama dva-apa (dvipa), Hapta-dvipa, s'śasma (śuśoma) Apaga* find place in seals. The ranking of protector or saviour, who may be an earthly or heavenly being, is quite clear, e.g. *paka* (guardian) *pa/pat* (protector), *s'āsa* (ruler), *pat-pat* (great protector), and *śāsa-śāsa* (great ruler) are noteworthy. In short, it can be said that even when determinatives, ideographs and phonetised pictures were dropped in purely cursive writing, the texts refer to seeking protection or praising the saviour. Hence, it is difficult to classify the early writing as hieratic or official and the later one as commercial as suggested by Dani. The religious context is obvious in a large number of inscriptions of both the periods. Whether the fish sign stood for a conjunct is not certain. It stood for *s'* which is equated to *xsa* in the *Avesta.*

According to S.S. Misra, Indo-Iranian signifies a stage when Indo-Aryan and Iranian were not independent dialects. The strong linguistic affinity of Indo-Aryan and Iranian is the basis for such assumption. Old Iranian comprises Avestan and Old Persian. Avestan was the language of Eastern Iran recorded in the sacred book of the Parsis called *Avesta*, written in avestan script and Old Persian was the language of western and south-western Iran attested in the cuneiform inscription of the Achaemenian emperors. As a rule, all final vowels which have become long in Gothic and Avestan are to be pronounced short. This is true of Indus language to a large extent, e.g. *Mahā, Bakā, Bhagā,* etc.

AVESTA

The three sacred verses of the Avesta are: 1. *Yatha ahu vairyo,* 2. *Asam vohu,* and 3. *Yenhe hatam.* These three prayers (C. Dutta 1973, 1) are the most famous of the ancient verses of Iran. All the three are of great antiquity perhaps of pre-Zarathustra age. *Ahuna-Vairya* is the oldest having the same antiquity as the *Gāyatri* for the Hindus. According to Taraporewala, the clue to interpretation of *Ahuna vairya* is given by three names, viz., *Ahu, Vahumana* and *Xsathra. Ahuna Vairya* gives us the essentials of a life lived for the good of humanity and of service to mankind. The first line lays down the general proposition which is true of all religions that the spiritual teacher Ratu (*rta* in sanskrit) is all powerful just as earthly prince (Ahu) may be in the world. The reason for the power of the Ratu is his *Aśa*. The *Aśa* represents the divine will in manifestation, the law of God (law of purity and righteousness). *Asat* originally meant law or truth, the order in creation somewhat like the conception of *dharma* in India. Sometimes *Aśa* is personified as a divinity having a definite place in the divine hierarchy.

A.H. Dani, a renowned scholar in Sanskrit, after going through my book *Decipherment of Indus script* (1982) made some observations before my subsequent publication, *Dawn and Devolution of Indus Civilisation* (Aditya Prakashan, Delhi, 1991, pp. 200 to 284) in which I have dealt with the Indus script and language comprehensively. Dani says,

> I think your methodcology is far better than those who are busy with computers. I fully agree with your approach to get at the basic signs and subsidiary signs but I do not agree when you derive the value from the semitic. Semitic alphabets can be directly derived from pictographs of that region as the name of each semitic letter has a pictographic meaning.

In this connection what Driver has to say may be noted (*Semitic Writing*: G.R. Driver, 3rd Edn. 1976 ed., S.A. Hopkins, pp. 195-96). "The Phoenicians according to ancient tradition came from the shores of the Indian Ocean, including the Persian Gulf. Possibly they were a semitic tribe which reached the mediterranean coast as part of the same great movement which brought the Arameans and Hebrews to their historic homes in the west, and it is significant that the first mention of them occurs in Egyptian inscriptions in 1575 BC. It might therefore be conjectured that the Phoenicians, or a branch of them played a part, if not in the invention, at any rate in the transmission of the alphabet from the south to the north when the knowledge of it was spread far and wide by their commercial activity. As Greek and Latin historians averred, *They were certainly quick-witted and practical enough to see the advantages of the new invention and to turn it to their own use but probably not culturally gifted enough to make so remarkable a discovery even if that were chronologically possible. They were adapters rather than inventors. Yet here again as so often in life the genius who makes the discovery is often forgotten, while his successor, who turns it to practical use, gives his name to it.*" The Phoenicians (Phanis mentioned in the *Rigveda*) who were trading with Indus people seem to have taken advantage of the simplified Indus cursive script with 24 alphabets for commercial purpose. They took 15 consonantal signs with their phonetic value to write their consonantal script (Fig. 58). In the process, the very existence of the Indus civilisation and its alphabetic writing was forgotten for more than 3500 years until the cities of Harappa and Mohenjodaro were discovered in 1922 and the Harappan port of Lothal in 1955. The evolution of partly pictorial Indus script into a purely cursive alphabetic script (Fig. 58) by 1700 BC has been traced

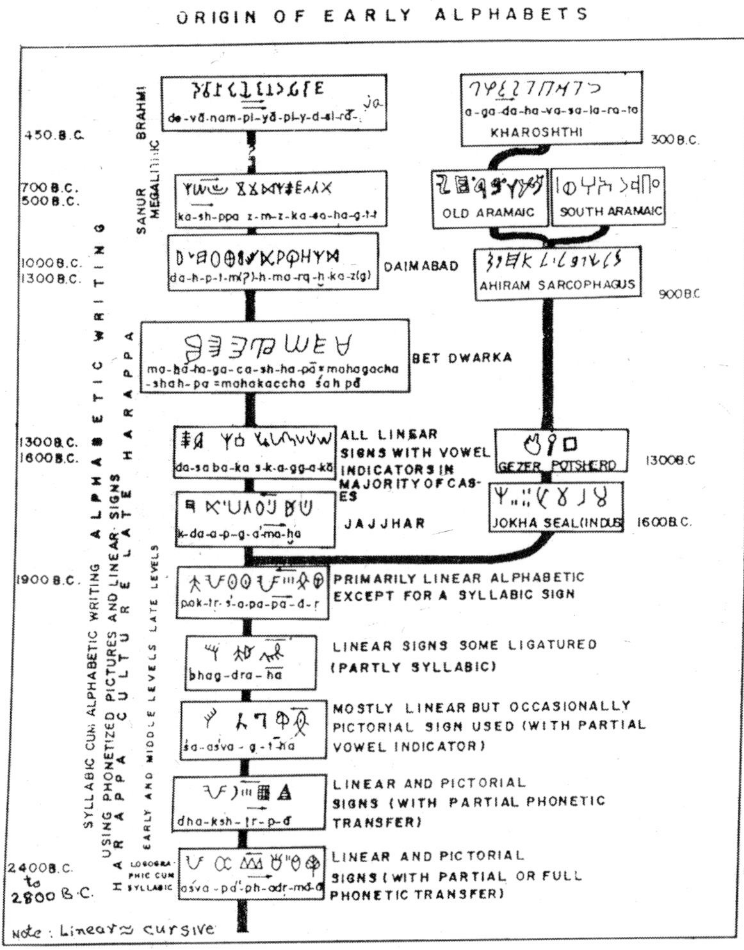

Fig. 58. Origin of early alphabets.

in late levels of almost all major Harappan sites including Lothal (Rao 1991), Harappa and Mohenjodaro (Dales 1987-88 and 1965).

The Sumero Accadian cuneiform script contains over 550 signs of which 285 may be used as syllabic signs or letter signs. The Egyptian hieroglyphs are over 700 in number, of which some 70 to 100 may be used syllabically and 24 may be used alphabetically with letter values. The Ugaritic and South Semitic alphabets have 26 to 29 letters and the Arabic alphabet has 28 letters against the 22 letters of the Phoenic Aramaico Hebrew alphabet.

INDUS AND BRAHMI SCRIPTS

The chronological gap between the Harappan cursive script (1600 BC) and Brahmi script (400 BC) is now partly bridged by the TL dating of the Bet Dwarka inscriptions of 16th century BC in which the evolved cursive Harappan script is written in a rightward direction unlike the Indus leftward script. It is now possible to suggest that several Brahmi alphabetic signs are derived from the late Harappan cursive signs. The inscription in evolved Indus script in the unicorn seal from Jokha (Fig. 58) datable to 6th century BC serves as one more link between late Indus and Brahmi scripts.

SALIENT FEATURES OF THE INDUS LANGUAGE

The Harappans resorted to doubling of consonants for emphasis or for some other reason, which the Vedic grammrians, namely, the *prātiśākhyas* also continued. The first member of a consonant group if preceded by a vowel, should be doubled for example, *aśśvinorrvvāhubhyām*. The Mss (5350 of British Museum) of White *Yajurveda* consistently doubles the initial plosive consonant of every consonant group not only when preceded by a syllable belonging to the same word, e.g., *rakksah* but also when preceded by a separate word (e.g., *Upadāmi-bbhrātrvyaya*) *Vvanaspathyo-ggravaggravasi*. The Harappans also doubled the initial consonants, e.g., *ppaka, ttraṭa,* etc. as in MS 7350 of white *Yajurveda* (S.S. Misra, 62-70) and in Khotanese, an Indo-Aryan language. Indus language often uses an epithet twice *(dvitva)*, e.g., *pat - pat*, meaning great ruler or ruler of rulers (as in *Rv*, for example, divé divé).

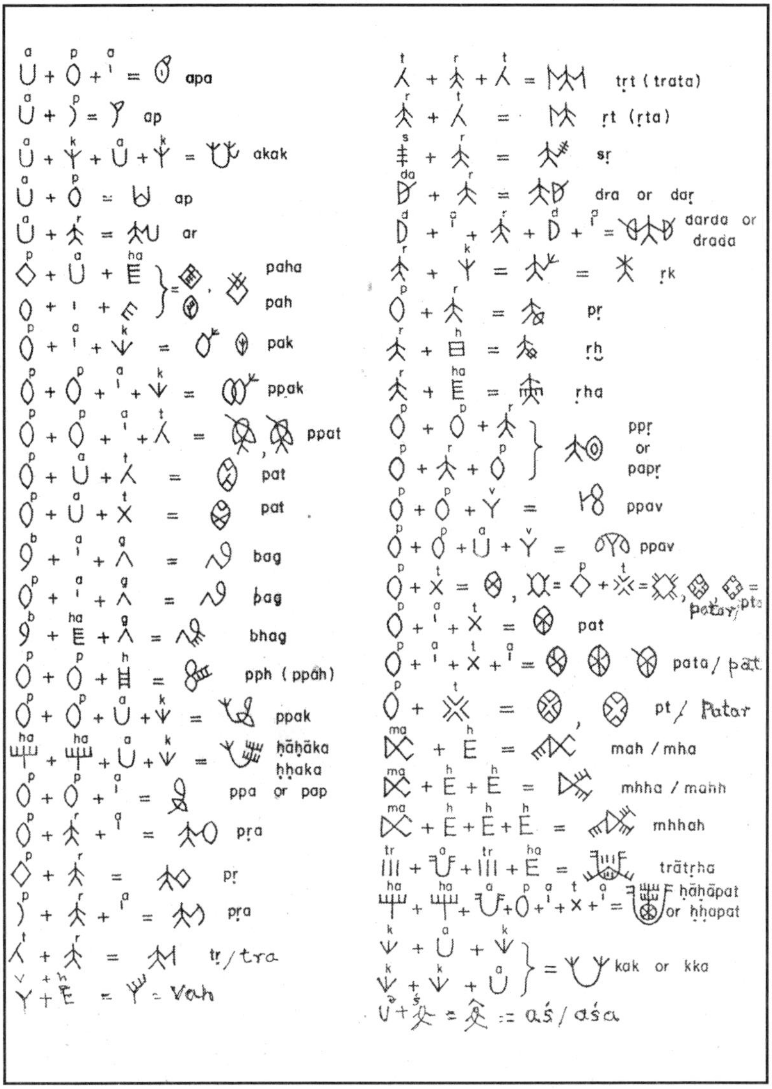

Fig. 59. Forming conjunct consonants and syllabic words by joining basic signs.

← INSCRIPTION	→ READING	MEANING
81. 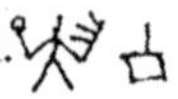	*barhay=barhi*	sacred grass, Agni (RV) *barazahi* upon highest height(AV) *barhas* height (AV)
82. 	*bag, baga*	deity, god, lord, divine power (AV)
83. 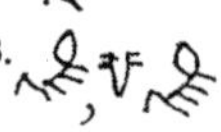	*bhag, bhaga*	*bhaga* dispenser, gracious lord, patron, good fortune, dignity, majesty, n of an Aditya (RV)
84. 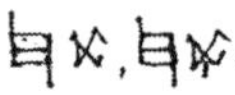	*maḫā, māḫa*	*maha* great, mighty, strong (RV)
85. 	*maḫa*	abundant (RV) *mas* great, large (AV) (originally *maz*)
86. 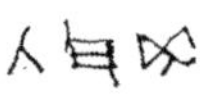	*mahat = mahat*	eminent (RV)
87. 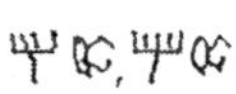	*maḥa = makha*	cheerful, a scrifice, n of a mythical person (RV)
88. 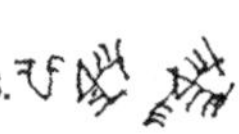	*mhha, mhahh*	*mahah* be great (RV) *makhah* sacrifice (RV)
89. 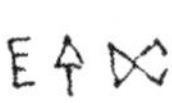	*madaha/madha*	*madh* deligh, enjoy, *mada* spiritous liquor (RV) *madhu* sweet (RV)
90. 	*mana*	*mana* a unit of weight
91. 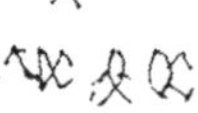	*maś*	great, large (AV)
92. 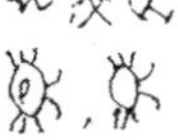	*makṣ*	*makṣ/makha* (logoram) cheerful (RV)

Fig. 60. Reading Indus inscriptions and their meaning.

INFLECTION

The inflexional character of the Indus language is indicated by the suffix *ā* for instrumental *ae/é* for dative and *h/ah* for genitive cases. The rare Harappan alternate ending *-ao/-o* and the *sandhi* form of *-as* are occassionally noticed.

VERBAL FORMS

There are several roots and a few past-participles comparable to the roots and participles of Vedic language. As many as 26 verbal bases common to IE stock and 41 common to OIA are traced in the Indus script.

NOMINAL COMPOUNDS

More than a hundred examples of *samāsa*, especially *Tatpuruṣa* and *Karmadharaya*, are identified in Indus inscriptions. But the commercial character of the inscriptions restrict the use of finite verbs. Mostly personal names, titles and honorofics such as ruler, protector, saviour, gracious, mighty, eminent, powerful and bounteous forming the *samāsa* are written.

SYNTAX

The frequent occurrence of adjectival forms in the post-position of nouns can be explained from the importance attached to the qualifying elements such as titles and honorofics as in *Śāsa mahā*, 'ruler great'. But there are also instances where the noun follows the adjective as in *Mahāśada* (greatly eminent), *Bhaga Arka* (bountiful), *Arka*, etc. In RV also there are several instances of adjectives following nouns.

ANIMAL MOTIFS ON SEALS

Deification of animals was very popular with the Harappans, for instance, the elephant and tiger have horns in seals to indicate their divinity.

Among the animals represented on seals, the unicorn seems to stand for the deified horse-cum-bull as indicated by horns. A few composite animals are also depicted. But the inscriptions are unrelated to the animals since different inscriptions are written on seals in which the same animal is depicted. The horned animals seem to be symbolic of nature deities. There are offering vessels in front of most animals. It is only in the case of the unicorn that the fire-altar occurs. In solitary instances there is an altar in front of a tiger or a goat.

INDUS AND INDO-EUROPEAN LANGUAGES

Among the Indo-European languages with which the language of Indus seals shows affinity, the Old Indo-Aryan (Vedic), Old Iranian (including Avestan), Old Persian and Hittite are noteworthy, but the degree of closeness of the Indus language in vocabularly, semantics, phonology and other grammatical features varies from language to language. It is closest to the language of the *Rigveda*, and to a limited extent, with the Old Iranian, its affinity with the Hittite language is least. What is however interesting is that the basic concepts about cosmology, society and state held by the Indus and *Rigvedic* people is almost identical. The Indus religion acts as a link between the Vedic and Avestan faiths. This is particularly true of the fire-cult of the Indus, Vedic and Iranian religions.

It is only by comparing certain Indus words like *mas, maḥa* and *maha (makha)* with the Old Persian-Avestan words that the subtle distinction in meaning, namely, great, bountiful, etc., becomes clear. Similarly, the words *sah, sahas,* and *śaka* used in Indus seals convey the sense, king, power and powerful, respectively. The terms for king, namely, *Kṣatra* and *sah*; for God *bag/bhaga*; for fire *atha/ata* (Vedic *Athar*) and for 'Lord' or Chief', *pat (pati* in Sanskrit) used in the Indus language are traceable in the Iranian tradition.

The Indus Valley writing is aphoristic in style like the *Sutras*. No full sentence is written on seals, substantives and qualifying elements are placed in no particular order as their position depended on the emphasis laid. No connecting link is traceable in several instances. The absence of gender and number indicator and a connecting element should be understood in the light of extreme brevity expected of the scribe to convey the sense through words which could be accomodated within the space of a couple of centimeters on the seal. Fortunately, the inflexional elements used in some inscriptions do suggest that the language was not agglutinative.

The Vedic vocabulary of the Harappan times is preserved in the seal inscriptions in the same way as the language of Yaska's time in the *Nirukta*. Just as the archaism of the Vedic language becomes apparent as we move from Yaska's *Bhāṣa* to the *Upaniṣads* and the *Brāhmaṇas*, the archaism of the Indus language becomes apparent from a comparative study of the Indus, Vedic and Avestan languages. In brief, it can be said that the Indus seal-texts are oldest treatises on phonology, etymology and syntax. They also serve as an important source for the study of comparitive religions.

Index